Cookie Jars BOOK II

Ermagene Westfall

Collector Books
A Division of Schroeder Publishing Co., Inc.

The current values in this book should be used only as a guide. They are not intended to set prices, which vary from one section of the country to another. Auction prices as well as dealer prices vary greatly and are affected by condition as well as demand. Neither the Author nor the Publisher assumes responsibility for any losses that might be incurred as a result of consulting this guide.

Searching For a Publisher?

We are always looking for knowledgeable people considered to be experts within their fields. If you feel that there is a real need for a book on your collectible subject and have a large comprehensive collection, contact Collector Books.

TABLE OF CONTENTS

DEDICATION

I would like to dedicate this book to my family. Earl Ray, my husband, has helped almost endlessly with the picture taking. Chantél, our youngest daughter, has helped with researching companies yet still preparing herself for her final year of high school. Our three older children, Dirinda, Geoffrey and Brock have given us four delightful grandchildren. Our grandchildren, Peyton Westfall, 8, Chelsea Lacen, 7, and Cameron Lacen, 4, have hardly ever gone to Grandma and Grandpa Westfall's house without being told "Watch out for that cookie jar," or "Don't knock that cookie jar off!" Sarah Westfall, who is just now three months old, doesn't even know what a cookie jar is but will undoubtedly be hearing the same thing before long!

Thanks for just being around and I love you each dearly.

Ermagene, Mom & Grandma.

ACKNOWLEDGMENTS

I've wondered many times since my first cookie jar book came out in 1983 if this second book was ever going to be. It seems like everything has gone wrong at every turn. We had trouble with the camera, the developers, and then even health problems became a factor, causing a big slow down. After years of persistence, though, it's finally ready to go to the publisher, to whom I want to give my first thanks.

Thanks to Bill Schroeder, who apparently still had faith in me, although the three or four years when I was to do another book has turned into almost ten.

Thanks to the following friends and collectors who have offered to help in special ways with this book.

Gari and Carl McCallum of California offered to take pictures of their jars for me. Several letters went back and forth between us as the McCallums communicated to me which jars they possessed, and I, in turn, communicated which jars I wanted them to photograph and with which jar. They supplied me with many pictures of California jars as well as some from other companies, which would not have otherwise been included in this book. I know there must have been times when they regretted ever offering such an undertaking, but I want them to know how very much I appreciate their help. I also want to let them know what a marvelous job they did on the photography; it couldn't have been any better! I hope when this book is in your hands, Gari and Carl, you will feel it's all been worthwhile.

Thanks to Martha and Bill Burleson of Indiana, who have shared their home with us again. We had gone there a few years ago to take pictures only to find our camera wasn't working, so we returned home, put the camera in the shop and eventually made a second trip to Indiana. Bill helped me carry jars back and forth across the huge cookie jar room that he has built. This room, let alone some of the jars, would make any cookie jar collector envious! They both accompanied us to the film developer, which undoubtedly would have taken us much longer to find alone since we were in an unfamiliar area. The friendship of both of you will always be treasured.

I'd like to thank Virginia and Hank Hanewinkle of Missouri, with whom we shared several nice visits and delicious meals while photographing their jars. Virginia and Hank have a home on the lake, so they have jars on two levels. They let me take complete charge, going from room to room and upstairs or downstairs to get the jars I wanted to photograph. Hank has built shelves over the stairs from the lake level to the top floor, and he had to get a ladder to get some jars down and then put back. I was going to just leave them out of the book, but Hank insisted he had been a carpenter and it was not a problem. I was the one who was scared he might fall. You guys are great!

Mammie Wiegers of Nebraska also deserves my words of gratitude. Mammie has been collecting jars longer than anyone I know. I have been collecting for 35 years, but Mammie started before that! Walron, Mammie's husband, is every bit as proud of her collection as she is. Sometimes, I think the husbands get more involved in these collections than the partners who started it. Thanks for sharing an afternoon of photography with us.

Jody Bay, Evlyn Wolf and Richard Renn from Missouri all loaned me jars to bring to our home to photograph. One of Jody's jars even went to Indiana with us. How many collectors would let you borrow a jar and then skip the state with it? Evlyn Wolf also loaned jars to me to photograph for my first book. Thanks to each of you!

Linda Waite of Arizona sent me pictures of jars, which you will be seeing. Thanks Linda! Connie and Wayne Brown of Texas shared jars with us. They brought them when they visited Connie's folks, left them, and then picked them up on their next trip. It was appreciated.

Thanks to Alene Maloney, Elinor and Jim Tuggle, Linsey and Frank Grismore, Betty and Freddy Hunter and Martha and Gerald McCann, all from Missouri. They all shared a jar!

To each and every one of the above, whether I photographed one jar or several, this book would not have been as complete as what it is without your help, although no book is ever complete. I know your jars will give the other collectors hours of enjoyment.

Thanks to the following people who have provided me with information! Ann Davin of Connecticut, Peter Minot of Arizona, Don Winton of California, Mary Allen of West Virginia and Carolyn Castillion of Tennessee.

I believe I owe an apology to Jean McElroy of Illinois. I believe Jean had sent me pictures of Peter Max for my book, but due to the fact I received so many letters and pictures from collectors, some wanting to sell their jars and some just to share, I got her mixed up with someone else and sent the pictures back. Jean, I'm sorry! Please forgive me.

PREFACE

Cookie jar collecting is a steadily growing hobby. Who would have thought several years ago that there would be so many collectors? Or better yet, who would have ever thought there would be so many cookie jars?

The sad part of collecting now is that so many of the American pottery companies are no longer in business. Although the foreign made jars are quite pretty, they can never compare to the American made ones for both durability and beauty combined. With the McCoy Company no longer in business, as of last year, and the closing of Regal China this year, that leaves but a few American pottery (or ceramic) companies still in operation. Even the older crockery type jars with hand decorated flowers or fruit, which I have always liked, will become highly collectible or so I believe. Even now, the tall "Milk Can" type are often used without the lids to hold kitchen utensils. You know, the housewives in earlier days must have been just as thrilled to see a cookie jar decorated in that way as we are nowadays when we see something new.

I've heard many people comment at flea markets as they go past a cookie jar booth that Andy Warhol's auction is what turned cookie jar collecting "ON." I disagree. It may have enticed a few more to start collecting, but I know of many, including myself, who were collecting long before they knew who Andy Warhol was.

Although Shawnee Pottery is what really got me started collecting in 1957, I could no longer say it is my favorite pottery. If someone would put all of the American Pottery company names in a hat, draw one out, I would immediately think of a jar made by that company that I wouldn't dream of giving up.

I have often wondered just exactly what the lettering "GOB" means on the Shawnee gold trimmed sailor. I do know that was a name the sailors were called, but even when members of our families have been in the Navy, no one seems to know. Which brings this to my mind. I have wondered if maybe it wasn't "Godbless Our Boys." Of course, I'm sure other people might think of some other meaning.

I read in the Roerig book about Joyce trying to take the paint off a red colored Winnie. Well, let me tell you another similar story. After two weeks of hand sanding as well as my husband using an electric sander, we got the job done. My fingers were sore for a long time. It's amazing that it took all that time and effort just to find that it was supposed to be there all the time! I sanded in the crease where he couldn't use the sander. We all have learned, haven't we? I remember telling Joyce about that when we were in Texas once, but she didn't give me a clue that she had tried it too.

Some jars are listed in this book again as unknown. I do have my belief on some of them but cannot say for sure. I believe the big whale with Pinocchio is a Starnes because I think Starnes used more grays than any other pottery company.

How many of you have noticed the differences in the Little Red Riding Hoods as far as color? The older cream ones were naturally the older, but the newer, whiter ones do not have the glaze on the inside of the head as the ones marked HULL WARE. I wonder if Regal China decorated these jars for Hull, and produced them as well, when the Hull factory burned and wasn't yet rebuilt. My reason for thinking this is because so many, if not most, of the Regal China jars are not glazed on the inside of the lids.

Seasonal jars are hard to find, and probably for that very reason they are seasonal. Once used for the holiday, the jars are probably packed away with other holiday decorations. That's why, in my opinion, they are scarce.

Not only do I collect cookie jars, but I used to collect cookbooks. The Helen's Tat-L-Tale which is pictured on the front of this book is shown in the Mary Margaret McBride cookbook (which was bought in sections at the Safeway store back in the 1960's). This at least gives us some clue as to how old that jar is. We know it must have been around in the 50's. Many of the older cookie jars are pictured in some of the advertising pamphlets, too.

A different McCoy-Betsy Baker is pictured in this book than what was in my first, but I know there is yet another. I haven't found it yet, but. . . ?

We thought the American Pottery Companies were confusing by so many of the companies using the same molds. Well, the same thing is going to hold true with the foreign companies. I have already found that the Ninja Turtles not only were made in Taiwan, but Korea as well. However, they are issued by the same company.

What used to always be Enesco Imports Japan, also has jars out that read Enesco Imports Taiwan. It is nearly impossible to keep the American Potteries separate, but with the imports, it is impossible. Many are only marked with stickers. Once that sticker or label is gone . . . ?

Many of the older and hard to find jars are now being copied and in some cases the maker/makers even have permission to use the company mark (although the company is out of business). I am not pleased about these reproductions as I feel they hurt collections when many collectors have paid premium prices for original jars. I feel the reproductions will indeed make the prices of the original jars decrease in value.

Many collectors ask me about purchasing damaged jars. I do, if I don't have that jar or know it is a hard one to find. When and if I get a chance to up-date it, I will. It is not always possible to find perfect cookie jars, especially the older ones, with this many collectors around.

I feel like a collector should buy what he likes, pay what he thinks it worth to him and display it with pride.

ABINGDON POTTERY

The Abingdon Pottery began as the Abingdon Sanitary Manufacturing Company in Abingdon, Illinois, in 1908, with Raymond E. Bidwell as President. Bidwell retired in 1948 and John M. Lewis who had been Vice-President emerged as President. By 1934, art pottery was beginning to be made. Thus, in 1939, the cookie jars that we collectors are still collecting today, came into production.

The name of the company was changed to Abingdon Pottery in 1945. By 1950, sixteen different cookie jars had been produced. Several, such as the Little Old Lady, for example, were made in solid colors and some with various trim and/or decorations. The Little Old Lady was also the first cookie jar Abingdon produced.

1950 also saw the closing of the Abingdon Pottery. In 1951 the plant was sold, and was again to be used for manufacturing sanitary ware.

Little Old Lady: Marked:
"Abingdon USA 471"
$195.00 – $215.00
Little Old Lady: Marked:
"Abingdon USA 471"
$200.00 – $225.00

Little Old Lady: Marked:
"Abingdon USA 471"
$150.00 – $175.00
Little Old Lady: Marked:
"Abingdon USA 471"
$140.00 – $160.00

Little Girl: Marked:
"Abingdon USA 693"
$95.00 – $100.00
Daisy Jar: Marked:
"Abingdon USA 677"
$80.00 – $90.00

Hippo Bar Jar: Marked:
"Abingdon USA 549"
$300.00 – $325.00
Hippo with Yellow Flower:
(Have seen this with bright red
flower and bold red lipstick)
Marked: "Abingdon USA 549"
$225.00 – $250.00

Little Miss Muffet: Marked:
"Abingdon USA 622"
$210.00 – $240.00
Jack-O-Lantern: Marked:
"Abingdon USA 674"
$325.00 – $350.00

Fat Boy: Marked: "Abingdon USA 495"
$200.00 – $225.00
Jack-O-Lantern: "674" If this jar is stamped with Abingdon Mark, it doesn't show up because of the dark green color.
$250.00 – $275.00

Train: Marked: "Abingdon USA 651"
$150.00 – $165.00
Windmill: Marked: "Abingdon USA 678"
$225.00 – $250.00

Train: Marked: "Abingdon USA 651"
$150.00 – $165.00
Plaid Jar (Abingdon look-a-like):
This jar unmarked:
$20.00 – $30.00
Abingdon one $50.00 – $60.00

ALBERTA'S MOLDS, INC.

Many different companies made molds of various items to be sold and used in ceramic shops. Alberta's was just one of many. I do believe in this case though, one of these jars was company made. The green rocking horse was a gift to me from our oldest daughter for Christmas one year. She bought it at a Drugstore & Gift Shop. The beige horse was bought at a flea market and does not show the quality as far as clay used nor the coloring. The beige looks as if it was made at a ceramic shop or class.

Green Rocking Horse: Marked:
"Alberta's Molds, Inc. 1956"
$40.00 – $50.00
Beige Rocking Horse: Marked:
"Alberta's Molds, Inc. 1956"
$12.00 – $15.00

ALLADIN PLASTICS, INC.

Alladin Plastics, Inc., was founded by Sam Avadon around 1945 at Gardena, California. The plant in Gardena was the only plant until 1965 when Mr. Avadon decided to build a plant on the East Coast to broaden the market. The plant was built in Surgoinsville, Tennessee. Later, Mr. Avadon sold the plant and retired. The company has since had two ownerships.

Alladin Plastic, Inc., was a subsidiary of Lenox for a number of years until the present owner, Mr. Charles Carson, bought it in the late '70's or early '80's. The company presently has two plants: one in Gardena, California, and the other in Sugoinsville, Tennessee, which is the corporate headquarters.

Paddys Pig: Unmarked:
$35.00 – $40.00
Paddys Pig: Unmarked:
$35.00 – $40.00

AMERICAN BISQUE COMPANY

The American Bisque company of Williamstown, West Virginia was founded in 1919 by A.W. Ridge, W. Eberle and King McCrury. Their intended purpose was to manufacture bisque and china doll heads.

A man who had been an investor in the company, Mr. B.E. Allen, purchased all the stock in 1922. After World War I, the company began to produce various pottery items, which included many cookie jars.

Following the purchase of the company by B.E., it was owned and operated by the Allen Family including B.E., his son Neal, and grandson Charlie. I was informed by a member of the Allen Family that the company ceased production in 1979.

I received a letter from a member of the American Bisque family in September of 1988 informing me as to some jars their company made that I had listed as "unknown" in my first book. Information such as this is always welcome. So many times this is the only way a person has of indentifying certain jars, especially since so many different companies use the same molds.

Policeman: Unmarked: $110.00 – $140.00
Note! Hat reads police, but on back of collar is "Cop."
Pirate: Unmarked: $110.00 – $140.00

Soldier: Unmarked: **Note!** Barracks hat. Much harder to find than other of the Roly-Poly jars or so to speak. $175.00 – $225.00
S.S. Kookie: Unmarked: $90.00 – $100.00

World War II W.A.C. Head:
(US member of the Women's
Auxiliary Corps):
$80.00 – $100.00
Mismatched jar. W.A.V. E.
head, but W.A.F. hat. I have
priced this jar as though it
was complete since the hats
often were switched, broken
or used on other jars.
$80.00 – $100.00

World War II W.A.V.E.S. Head:
US Naval reserve. (Women's
Appointed Volunteer Emergency
Service) Unmarked:
$80.00 – $100.00
Davy Crockett coming out of
Forest: Unmarked:
$825.00 – $1,000.00

World War II W.A.F.
Head: (US Member of the
Women's Air Force) **Note!**
This jar has been glazed.
I've only seen two with the
glaze. Unmarked:
$80.00 – $100.00
Soldier: (Blue mustache)
Unmarked:
$80.00 – $100.00

Soldier: (Black mustache)
Unmarked:
$80.00 – $100.00
Professor or colonel?
Unmarked:
$80.00 – $100.00

Soldier: Unmarked:
$160.00 – $190.00
Sailor: Unmarked:
$160.00 – $190.00

Pirate: Unmarked:
$75.00 – $90.00
Sailor: Unmarked:
$75.00 – $90.00

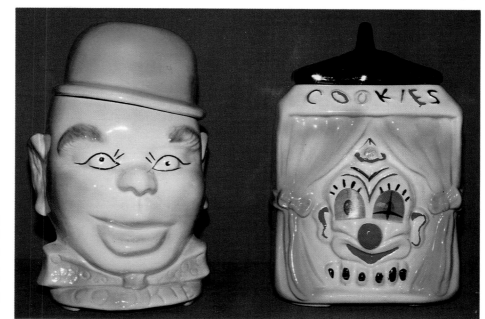

Pinky Lee: Unmarked: Ungemach
$350.00 – $450.00
Clown on Stage:
Clown has flasher eyes.
Marked: "805 USA"
$275.00 – $330.00

Clown on Stage:
Clown has flasher eyes.
Marked: "805 USA"
$275.00 – $330.00
Clown on Stage:
Clown has flasher eyes.
Marked: "805 USA"
$275.00 – $300.00

Tortoise & Hare:
Hare has flasher face:
Marked: "803 USA"
$275.00 – $325.00
Bear with Bee-Hive:
Bear has flasher face:
Marked: "804 USA"
$275.00 – $325.00

Sandman Cookies:
Note! Different T.V. scene than in first book. Clown has flasher face:
Marked: 801 USA
$250.00 – $300.00
Cow Jumped Over the Moon:
Moon has flasher face:
Marked: "806 USA"
$375.00 – $450.00

Girl Bear: Marked: "USA"
$70.00 – $80.00
Boy Bear with cap & neckerchief:
Marked: "USA"
$70.00 – $80.00

Sleeping Bear: Unmarked:
$65.00 – $75.00
Cookie Jar with Recessed Base:
Note! This jar has a different mark than any other American Bisque jar I have ever seen. The mark is a circle about the size of a quarter in 22 K gold and "American Bisque Co. USA" is written in the circle also in 22 K gold. It is marked "22K gold" also plain "USA" incised on bottom.
$40.00 – $50.00

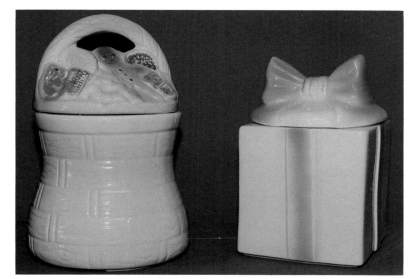

Basket of Cookies: Marked: "USA"
$50.00 – $55.00
Gift (or present): Marked: "USA"
$65.00 – $70.00

Winking Santa:
Marked: "USA"
$350.00 – $400.00
Rudolph: Marked:
"R L M (c)" The book was
written by Robert L. May for
Montgomery Ward. c. 1939.
I assume this jar was made
around that time for
Montgomery Ward.
$375.00 – $425.00

Rabbit in Yellow Hat: Marked: "USA"
$85.00 – $100.00
Rabbit in Green Hat: Marked: "USA"
$85.00 – $100.00

Granny Rabbit: Marked: "USA"
$150.00 – $175.00
Spool of Thread with Thimble & Needle:
Marked: "USA"
$100.00 – $120.00

Waving Clown: Marked: "USA"
$60.00 – $70.00
Chick with Tam: Marked: "USA"
$80.00 – $95.00

Clown: Unmarked:
$90.00 – $100.00
Clown: Unmarked:
$90.00 – $100.00
These clowns have the American Bisque
wedges and colors.
I also have the same clown listed again under
American Pottery as it is the American
Pottery blue.

Pennsylvania Dutch Farm Boy: Unmarked:
$275.00 – $300.00
Pennsylvania Dutch Girl: Unmarked:
$275.00 – $300.00

Puppy on Tucked Pillow:
Marked: "USA"
$60.00 – $75.00
Kitten on Tucked Pillow:
Marked: "USA"
$60.00 – $75.00

Poodle: Ungemach Marked: "USA CT5"
$125.00 – $150.00
Cat: Ungemach Marked: "USA"
$125.00 – $150.00

Churn Boy: Marked: "USA"
$200.00 – $225.00
Peasant Girl: Unmarked:
$350.00 – $400.00

Elephant with Sailor Hat:
Unmarked:
$70.00 – $80.00
Elephant with Patch on
Pants: Marked: "USA"
$80.00 – $90.00

Treasure Chest: Marked:
"USA"
$150.00 – $175.00
Dutch Boy: Marked: "USA"
$90.00 – $100.00

Cookie Bus: Marked: "USA"
$65.00 – $80.00
Puppy with Toothache:
Marked: "USA"
$750.00 – $775.00

Chef Head with Serving Tray
for Lid: Marked: "603 USA"
$325.00 – $350.00
Basket with Serving Tray for
Lid: Marked:
"601 USA"
$150.00 – $200.00

Yard Lantern: Marked:
"USA"
$125.00 – $140.00
Oak Leaves Corner Jar:
Marked: "USA"
$125.00 – $150.00

Fawn: Unmarked:
$90.00 – $100.00
Rocket-Ship:
Marked: "USA"
$600.00 – $650.00

Train Engine: Marked: "USA"
$90.00 – $100.00
Liberty Bell: Marked: "USA"
$125.00 – $150.00

Paddle Boat:
Marked: "USA"
$175.00 – $200.00
Cookie R.R.:
Marked: "USA"
$45.00 – $50.00

Herman & Katnip:
Marked: "USA" on back
of base, also stamped on
bottom of jar, "Famous
Harvey Cartoons 1960."
$3,000.00 – $3,200.00
Small Rabbit
with Paws in Pockets:
(about 9½")
Unmarked:
$90.00 – $95.00

Small Rabbit with Paws in Pockets:
(about 9½") Unmarked:
$90.00 – $95.00
Small Cat with Paws in Pockets:
(about 9½") Unmarked:
$90.00 – $95.00

Elephant with Forefeet in Pocket:
(about 9½") Unmarked:
$90.00 – $95.00
Rabbit with Paws in Pockets:
(about 9½") Unmarked:
$90.00 – $95.00

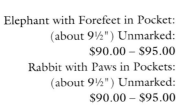

Elephant with
Forefeet in Pockets:
Marked: "USA"
$55.00 – $70.00
Elephant with
Forefeet in Pockets:
Marked: "USA"
$55.00 – $70.00

Davy Crockett: Marked: "USA"
$400.00 – $450.00
Indian Boy: Unmarked:
$1,250.00 – $1,500.00

Polka Dots: Marked: "Pat. Appd for USA"
$25.00 – $30.00
Puppet: Ungemach: Marked: "USA"
$55.00 – $70.00

Jar with Cookies, Pretzel Finial:
Marked: "USA"
$35.00 – $40.00
Gray Poodle: Marked: "USA"
$125.00 – $140.00

Lady Pig with Gold Trim: Unmarked:
$175.00 – $200.00
Red Poodle: Marked: "USA"
$125.00 – $140.00

Oaken Bucket with Gourd Dipper:
Marked: "USA"
$75.00 – $90.00
African Violet Jar: Marked: "USA"
$30.00 – $35.00

Yarn Doll: Unmarked:
$100.00 – $120.00
Yarn Doll: Unmarked:
$100.00 – $120.00

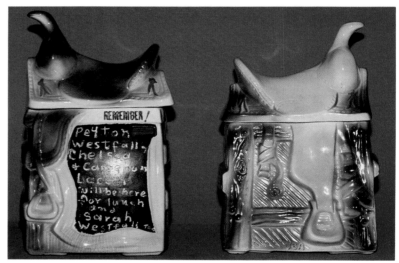

Blackboard Saddle: Marked: "USA"
$280.00 – $310.00
Saddle: Marked: "USA"
$260.00 – $290.00

Flying Blue Birds: Unmarked:
$30.00 – $35.00
Brown-Eyed Susan Flower: Marked:
"USA"
$30.00 – $35.00

Cookie Sack: Marked:
"USA 201"
$35.00 – $40.00
Cookie Girl with Braids:
Marked: "USA 202"
$40.00 – $46.00

Cookie Time Clock with
Gold Trim: Marked:
"USA 203"
$60.00 – $65.00
Cookie Girl with Braids—
Gold Trim: Marked:
"USA 202"
$65.00 – $70.00

Shy Lady Pig: Unmarked:
$95.00 – $110.00
Boy Pig: Marked: "USA"
$90.00 – $95.00

Clown with Cookies: Unmarked:
Note! Check this color against the same
mold on the clowns a few pages back and
with the color of the American Pottery
Company's two face pig. (on page **30**)
$90.00 – $100.00
Girl Pig: Unmarked:
$95.00 – $110.00

Wilma Flintstone: Marked: "USA"
$1,200.00 – $1,500.00
Fred Flintstone: Marked: "USA"
$1,500.00 – $1,800.00

Dino: Marked: "USA"
$1,400.00 – $1,600.00
Rubbles House: (Not shown) Marked:
"USA"
$1,000.00 – $1,200.00
Feed Sack: Marked: "USA"
$50.00 – $75.00

Popeye the Sailor Man: Unmarked:
$1,000.00 – $1,200.00
Olive Oyl: (Not shown) Marked: "USA"
$1,400.00 – $1,600.00
Sweet Pea (Not shown)
$1,800.00 – $2,000.00

Sea Bag: Marked: "USA"
$400.00 – $500.00

Apple with Bloom:
Unmarked:
$35.00 – $40.00
Ball Shape with Apple
on Limb: Marked:
"USA Pippin"
$35.00 – $40.00

AMERICAN POTTERY COMPANY

American Pottery Company began as Stoin-Lee Pottery at Marietta & Byesville, Ohio, in 1942. Later that same year, the name was changed to American Pottery, and headquarters moved to Marietta, Ohio, with J. Lenhart as owner.

While researching the American Pottery Company, many names appeared such as John Bonistall, who had been president of the Shawnee Company until its closing, and A.N. Allen of the American Bisque Company. J. Lenhart, owner of the company, was also connected with the American Bisque Company, and A.N. Allen shared responsibilities with the American Pottery Company.

This is undoubtedly why we cookie jar collectors are having trouble distinguishing between the two companies. Both companies made some jars from the same molds and sometimes the glaze on a jar is so thick the marks are illegible. I understand that hard feelings developed between the owners of the companies over some of the molds being used. So who had which mold first is difficult to determine.

Girl Lamb: Unmarked:
$140.00 – $160.00
(Two faced jar.
Reverse shown below)
Girl Pig: Unmarked:
$125.00 – $150.00
(Two faced jar.
Reverse shown below)

Bull: (Reverse side of lamb shown above)
Unmarked:
$140.00 – $160.00
Boy Pig: (Reverse side of lady pig shown above)
Unmarked:
$125.00 – $150.00

ANCHOR HOCKING GLASS COMPANY

Amber Sandwich Glass:
Unmarked:
$75.00 – $90.00
Clear Sandwich Glass: This
one being a reissue.
Unmarked:
$40.00 – $45.00

AVON PRODUCTS, INC.

Avon Products, Inc. was first known as the California Perfume Company, in 1886, headed by David McConnell.

Avon now has claim to a few cookie jars. However, the cookie jars Avon has given as awards to their representatives or that were sold to their customers were not made by the Avon Company, but contracted out to different ceramic companies. The company headquarters is now located in Martin Grove, Illinois.

Bear: Unmarked: $60.00 – $65.00
Spatterware Bear: Marked: "Avon" $55.00 – $60.00

Hen with Egg: Marked:
"Gallery Originals" $55.00 – $60.00

BAUER POTTERY

J.A. Bauer and his family began Bauer Pottery in Los Angeles, California, in 1905, although the company didn't begin making dinnerware until the early 30's. Bauer was the first to bring forth the mix-match varieties of the bright colored dinnerware.

Bauer Pottery's years of trade were completed at the 1950 death of J.A. Bauer.

Bauer Jar: Marked: "Bauer
USA Los Angeles"
$40.00 – $55.00

BRAYTON and/or BRAYTON LAGUNA POTTERY

Brayton or Brayton Laguna Pottery (you will find pieces marked both ways, as well as some unmarked) was founded in 1927 by Durlin Brayton at Laguna Beach, located in California.

The Brayton pottery items were first displayed in Brayton's yard, which was eye catching to many people, and later developed into a booming business. The business began to decline after Brayton's death in 1951 although employees tried to keep it going, and the Brayton Pottery expired in 1968.

The Brayton mammy cookie jars are highly sought after and are being copied by ceramists today.

Pretzel Jar: Marked: (With stamp)
"Brayton California USA"
also "H" incised.
$60.00 – $70.00
Animal Cookies:
Marked: (With stamp)
"Brayton California USA" also
"40" and "50" incised.
$75.00 – $85.00

Mammy with Red Dress:
(Bottom is not glazed)
Marked: "Brayton (c)" on bottom,
also "8" inside of lid rim.
$1,500.00 – $1,800.00
Mammy with Yellow Dress:
(Bottom is glazed)
Marked: "Copyright 1943 Brayton
Laguna Pottery" also "7"
$1,100.00 – $1,400.00

Mammy with Blue Dress:
(Glazed Bottom)
Marked: "Copyright 1943 Brayton
Laguna Pottery" also "5" on outside rim
of lid. $1,100.00 – $1,400.00
Mammy w/White Skirt: (Bottom is not
glazed) Marked with "5" on bottom and
a "3" on outer rim of lid.
$1,200.00 – $1,500.00

Mammy with Green Dress: (Glazed bottom)
Marked: "Copyright 1943 by Brayton
Laguna Pottery" also "2"
$1,500.00 – $1,800.00
Gypsy Lady: Marked:
"Brayton Laguna Pottery" (Incised)
$275.00 – $300.00

Grandma: Marked:
"Brayton Laguna Pottery"
$375.00 – $425.00
Dutch Lady:
(Gathering Christmas dinner)
Marked:
"Brayton Laguna Pottery"
$500.00 – $550.00

Calico Dog:
Marked: "Brayton"
(Stamped)
$425.00 – $450.00
Calico Dog: Unmarked,
but probably had been
stamped at one time.
$425.00 – $450.00

Jamaican Lady: Marked:
"Brayton Laguna Calif. K-27"
$500.00 – $575.00
Gingerbread People:
Marked: "H-3"
$90.00 – $100.00

Russian Lady: Unmarked:
$525.00 – $570.00
Pretzel House with Gingerbread Men:
Unmarked:
$60.00– $75.00

House: Unmarked
Pfaltzgraff Pottery:
$100.00 – $125.00
Pretzel House with
Gingerbread Men:
(No green trim)
$60.00 – $75.00

The last four jars shown are all unmarked as far as the maker, but due to the quality, weight (on some) and the colors used, as well as the opinion of other collectors and myself, I have placed them under Brayton.

BRUSH POTTERY

The Brush Pottery was first founded in Zanesville, Ohio, by George Brush in 1907. The company was destroyed by fire in 1908. After the fire, George Brush went to work for J.W. McCoy and this resulted in a partnership between the two in later years. The partnership was to later be known as the Brush-McCoy Pottery.

In 1925, the McCoy name was dropped and once again was the Brush Pottery. During the latter forties and through 1971, the Brush Pottery produced the cookie jars that are so collectible today.

Brush Pottery had many employees and among them were the Twin Wintons, Ross and Don and a part-time ceramist named George Krause. Many of the Brush jars were designed by the Winton Brothers, and that is why some jars were marked with a "W" along with the numbers. Although I do not have this confirmed, I wonder if the same holds true with George Krause as some jars are marked with a "K" and number.

Clown: (Blue Pants) Marked: "W 22 Brush USA"
$230.00 – $255.00
Clown Bust: Unmarked:
$425.00 – $450.00

Clown: (Yellow Pants)
Marked: "W 22 Brush USA"
$195.00 – $215.00
Little Angel: Marked: "W 17 USA Brush"
$700.00 – $775.00

Formal Pig: Marked:
"W 7 USA"
$325.00 – $350.00
Formal Pig: Marked:
"W 7 USA"
$300.00 – $325.00

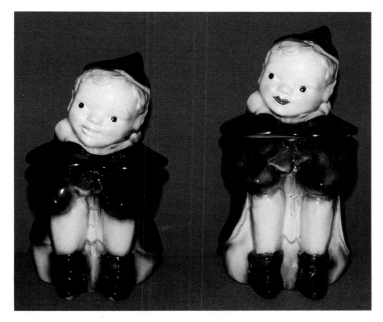

Peter Pan: Marked: "K 23 Brush USA"
$700.00 – $775.00
Peter Pan: Marked: "USA"
$800.00 – $900.00
Note! Lids will interchange on the two sizes.

Happy Squirrel: Marked:
"W 15 USA"
$225.00 – $250.00
Purple and White Cow:
Marked:
"Brush USA W 10"
$550.00 – $600.00

Brush

Granny with Rolling Pin:
Marked:
"W 19 Brush USA"
$225.00 – $250.00
Black and White Cow:
Marked:
"Brush USA W 10"
$800.00 – $1,000.00

Raggedy Ann: Marked: "W 16
USA"
$475.00 – $525.00
Balloon Boy: Unmarked:
$575.00 – $625.00

Gray House: Marked:
"W 31 Brush USA"
$65.00 – $75.00
Laughing Hippo: Marked:
"W 27 Brush USA"
$525.00 – $650.00

Sitting Hippo: Mismatched brush top with brush bottom: Unmarked: (Although this is mismatched, price is shown for a matched one) $475.00 – $500.00 Sitting Hippo: Unknown but shown here for comparison. $125.00 – $140.00

Blue and White Panda: Marked: "W 21 Brush USA" $400.00 – $450.00 Hobby Horse: Unmarked: $550.00 – $625.00

Donkey with Up-ended Cart: Marked: "W 33 Brush USA" $280.00 – $300.00 Squirrel on Log: Marked: "USA" $90.00 – $100.00

Gray Owl: Unmarked:
$100.00 – $125.00
Yellow Owl: Unmarked:
$95.00 – $115.00

Davy Crockett with Gold Trim:
Marked: "USA"
Note! I have never seen a larger
(Brush) Davy, although the Brush Red
Riding Hood, Little Boy Blue and
Peter Pan come in two sizes.
$500.00 – $525.00
Bear with Gold Trim: (Green pinafore)
Marked: "W 14 USA"
$575.00 – $625.00

Crockery Type with word "Cookies":
Unmarked:
$50.00 – $55.00
Crockery Type with Tulip: Unmarked:
$65.00 – $75.00

THE CALIFORNIA CLEMINSONS

Betty Cleminson began the "Cleminsons Clay" business in the garage of the Cleminsons' home at El Monte, California in 1941. The business first began as Betty's hobby, but soon became a family business and George, Betty's husband, was inducted to be in charge of the business affairs.

In 1943, the business outgrew the family garage and a new establishment was built. The name was then changed to "The California Cleminsons." The company thrived during the 40's and to the mid-50's, but with the impact of foreign imports during the early 60's, the Cleminsons could not compete their quality work with a compatable price of the foreign imports and the company closed in 1963.

Mother's Best: Marked: "The California Cleminsons" "Hand Painted" $200.00 – $225.00
Cookie House: Marked: "The California Cleminsons" "Hand Painted" $90.00 – $100.00

Cookie Book: Marked: "The California Cleminsons" "Hand Painted" $75.00 – $85.00
Card King: (Has spades, diamonds, hearts and clubs on his crown) Marked: "The California Cleminsons" "Hand Painted" $375.00 – $425.00

CALIFORNIA ORIGINALS ─────────────────

California Originals was founded in 1944 by William Bailey, first using a trade name—Heirlooms of Tomorrow. After World War II, the plant began an artware pottery operation which was sold under the name of California Originals. With a little less than three decades of operation, what was once known as the largest art pottery in the country, California Originals dissolved in 1982.

Big Bird with Rolling Pin:
Marked:
"MUPPETS, INC., 976"
$115.00 – $140.00
Ernie & Bert with
Cookie Monster: Marked:
"977 (c) 1971, 1978
MUPPETS, INC."
$275.00 – $300.00

Oscar the Grouch: Marked:
"(c) MUPPETS, INC., 972"
$75.00 – $80.00
Big Bird on Nest: Marked:
"(C) MUPPETS, INC., 971"
$90.00 – $100.00

Frog: (Too tired to croak) Marked: "877 USA"
$65.00 – $70.00
Sitting Frog: Marked: "2645 USA"
$50.00 – $55.00

Elves' School House: Unmarked:
$55.00 – $60.00
Snow White: Marked: "(c) Walt Disney Prod. 866 USA"
$525.00 – $600.00

Bear: (Highly glazed) Marked: "2648 USA"
$50.00 – $55.00
Bear: (Woodtone finish) Marked: "2648 USA"
$55.00 – $60.00

Elephant: Marked: "2643"
$50.00 – $55.00
Shoe House: Marked: "874 USA"
$35.00 – $40.00

Wonder Woman: Marked:
"USA 847 D.C. Comics, Inc., 1978"
$425.00 – $475.00
Superman: Marked:
"Cal Orig. USA 876 D.C. Comics Inc., 1978"
$400.00 – $450.00

Superman: Marked:
"Cal Orig. USA 876 D.C. Comics, Inc., 1978"
$425.00 – $475.00
Christmas Tree: Marked: "873"
$200.00 – $225.00

Cookie Safe with Bull Dog:
Marked: "2030-1-2"
$35.00 – $40.00
Mouse with Cookie Bag:
Marked: "2630 USA"
$40.00 – $45.00

Scarecrow: Marked: "871 USA"
$175.00 – $190.00
Raggedy Ann: Marked: "859"
$65.00 – $70.00

Frog: Marked: "906 USA"
$30.00 – $35.00
Turtle with Flowers:
Marked: "842 USA"
$35.00 – $40.00

Turtle: (High glaze) Marked: "2635"
$35.00 – $40.00
Turtle: (Woodtone finish) Marked:
"2635 USA"
$35.00 – $40.00

Cookie Safe with Jack Rabbit:
Marked: "2630-1-2-"
$35.00 – $40.00
Big Dumb Clown: Marked: "213"
$60.00 – $65.00

Mr. Burn Toaster: Marked: "879 USA"
$60.00 – $65.00
Duck: Marked: "740 USA"
This jar is referred to by some as a duckbill
platypus, but as one can tell from the picture
this duck has wings and feathers.
$65.00 – $80.00

Rooster: Marked: "Cal. Orig U.S.A
1127"
$35.00 – $40.00
Brown Duck: Unmarked:
$50.00 – $55.00

Winking Owl: Marked: "856 USA"
$35.00 – $40.00
Alarm Clock: (Cookie Time) Marked:
"860"
$40.00 – $45.00

Cookie Crock: Marked: "862 USA"
$75.00 – $85.00
Juggler Clown: Marked: "876 USA"
$60.00 – $65.00

Pack Mule: Marked:
"2633 USA"
$140.00 – $165.00
Juggler Clown: Marked:
"876 USA"
$60.00 – $65.00

Cottage: Marked: "2754"
$35.00 – $40.00
Noah's Ark:
Marked: "881 USA"
$65.00 – $75.00

Cookie Shoppe: Marked:
"Calif. Orig. G 132-USA"
$45.00 – $50.00
Cookie Bakery: Marked: "863"
$45.00 – $50.00

Gingerbread House:
Marked: "857 USA"
$40.00 – $45.00
Clown Riding Elephant:
Marked: "896"
$45.00 – $50.00

Coffee Grinder: Marked: "861 USA"
$30.00 – $35.00
Tea Kettle: Marked: "737 USA"
$32.00 – $36.00

Squirrel on Stump: (High gloss)
Marked: "2620"
$30.00 – $35.00
Pinocchio: Marked: "California Orig. G-131
USA"
$425.00 – $475.00

Squirrel on Stump: Unmarked:
$30.00 – $35.00
Rabbit on Stump: Unmarked:
$30.00 – $35.00

Eeyore: Marked:
"901 (c) Walt Disney
Productions"
$400.00 – $425.00
Winnie the Poo with
Hunny Pot: Marked:
(In lid only) "907"
$160.00 – $175.00

Cylinder Jar with Mickey & Pluto Decal:
Marked: "1980 Walt Disney Productions"
$50.00 – $60.00
Penguin: Marked: "839"
$70.00 – $75.00

Rabbit with Cookie: Unmarked:
$40.00 – $45.00
Circus Wagon with Lion:
Marked: "2631 USA"
$40.00 – $45.00

Little Red School House:
Marked: "869"
$60.00 – $70.00
Locomotive:
Marked: "2268 USA"
$40.00 – $45.00

Space Cadet: Unmarked:
$85.00 – $95.00
Century 21 House: Marked:
"(c) 1978 Century 21 Real Estate
Corp.
Made in USA"
$275.00 – $300.00

The Century 21 House is unconfirmed at this time, but I believe California Originals because of colors used and some correspondence with the Century 21 Company.

CARDINAL CHINA COMPANY ────────

Cardinal China was not a manufacturing company, but a distribution center located in Carteret, New Jersey. Some, if not all, of the cookie jars that were distributed by the Cardinal China Company were indeed produced by the American Bisque Company. This, of course, is no great surprise to collectors, since all of the Cardinal China jars have the tell-tale wedges which are common on many of the American Bisque Jars.

Cookie Sack: Marked: "USA Cardinal" $35.00 – $40.00 Old Fashioned Wall Telephone: Marked: "Cardinal 311 USA" $60.00 – $70.00

Sad Clown: Marked: "Cardinal USA" $90.00 – $100.00 The Graduate: Marked: "Cardinal USA" $95.00 – $100.00

CUMBERLAND WARE

A trade name of Roman Ceramics.

Oliver Hardy: Unmarked:
$325.00 – $350.00
Stan Laurel: Unmarked:
$325.00 – $350.00

DeFOREST OF CALIFORNIA

Many of the pottery, or ceramic, companies began as hobbies. DeForest of California began the same way under the skillful hands of Margaret DeForest. Margaret began her business in 1950. Once she began to sell the ceramic items she had made, she needed more space, so the family moved to another home which had a four-car garage which was turned into a factory. The company became incorporated and Jack DeForest, Margaret's husband became president. The DeForests' two sons, John & Roger were also involved with the expansion and success of the company. In 1970, they could no longer compete with Japanese imports and the company went out of business. The companys last known address was Duarte, California.

Nite Owl: Marked:
"DeForest of Calif USA 5537"
$42.00 – $48.00
Monkey with Cookie: Marked:
"DeForest of Calif USA 51"
$65.00 – $75.00

Snow Capped Bird House: Marked:
"1959 (c) DeForest of California USA"
$90.00 – $100.00
Granny Rabbit: Marked (but with the Wm.
Hirsch mark:) WH © 58
$45.00 – $50.00

Pot of Cookies: Unmarked:
$30.00 – $35.00
Granny Rabbit: Marked:
"DeForest of California"
$38.00 – $42.00

Cloth Bear: Marked:
"1960 (c) DeForest of California USA"
$35.00 – $40.00
Monk: Marked:
"(c) 1964 DeForest of California USA"
$70.00 – $80.00

Cloth Bear: Marked:
"DeForest of Calif USA (c)
1964"
$55.00 – $60.00
Chipmunk: Marked:
"DeForest 514"
$55.00 – $60.00

Little Girl: Marked: "DeForest of
California (c) 1957"
$450.00 – $500.00
There is a matching boy to this jar.
Grandma, Knitting: Unmarked:
No proof this is DeForest, but
comparing colors etc. I feel that it is.
$150.0 – $175.00

Pig with Cookie: Marked:
"DeForest of Calif."
$70.00 – $80.00
Lamb: Unmarked:
(Check this lamb with T.W. ones.
This one has on apron-"For my
Little Lamb")
$55.00 – $60.00

Pig Head: Marked:
"DeForest of California"
"Hand Painted"
$45.00 – $50.00
Fortune Cookies: Marked:
"DeForest of Calif 5535
(c) 1957"
$60.00 – $65.00

DEE LEE OF CALIFORNIA

At this time, I have been unable to trace anything down on the Dee Lee Company. However, I have had items marked Dee Lee of Hollywood. The years in business and the location of the headquarters are uncertain to me.

DEMAND MARKETING

I was unable to find any information on the Demand Marketing Company. I do know it was in the late '70's when our son, Brock, gave me the set of three jars for Christmas.

Little Chef: Marked:
"Ceramica Primavera S.A."
$80.00 – $85.00

Big Bird: Marked: "Demand
Marketing.
Henderson, Ky. Made in USA
(c) MUPPETS, INC."
$45.00 – $50.00

Cookie Monster: Marked:
"Demand Marketing.
Henderson, Ky.
Made in USA
(c) MUPPETS, INC."
$45.00 – $50.00
Oscar the Grouch: Marked:
"Demand Marketing.
Henderson, Ky.
Made in USA
(c) MUPPETS, INC."
$45.00 – $50.00

DORANNE OF CALIFORNIA

Doranne of California Incorporated, began business in 1951. The company has produced extensive lines of art decorated pieces. Most of the cookie jars we have in our collection are marked with a letter or letters and a number or numbers. The company is located in Los Angeles.

Jeep: Marked: "USA J 54"
$75.00 – $80.00
Donkey with Cape:
Unmarked:
$80.00 – $90.00

Rabbit with Carrot:
Marked: "C J 106"
$55.00 – $65.00
Pig with Barrel:
Marked: "C J 105"
$55.00 – $65.00

Scottish Pig: Unmarked:
$50.00 – $55.00
Bear with Bee on Back:
Unmarked:
$50.00 – $55.00

Eggplant: Marked:
"C J 31 (c) USA"
$55.00 – $60.00
Crookneck Squash: Marked:
"C J 37 (c) USA"
$40.00 – $45.00

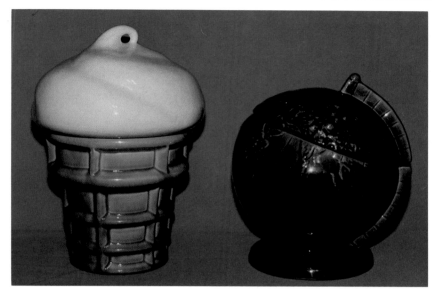

Ice Cream Cone: Marked: "J 57 USA"
$35.00 – $40.00
World Globe: (Green) Marked: "J 14"
$75.00 – $90.00

Bear Leaning Against
Mushroom: Unmarked:
$50.00 – $55.00
Bear with Bib: Unmarked:
$50.00 – $55.00

Fancy Cat: Marked: "J USA"
$40.00 – $45.00
Basset Hound: Marked: "J 1
USA"
$45.00 – $50.00

Baby Bird: Marked: "C J 6 USA"
$60.00 – $75.00
Leprechaun: Marked: "C J 42 USA"
$85.00 – $95.00

Dog with Bow: Unmarked:
$58.00 – $62.00
Sheep Dog: Unmarked:
$35.00 – $40.00

Elephant: Marked: "California"
$30.00 – $35.00
(Dande) Lion: Unmarked:
$45.00 – $50.00

Deer: Marked: Illegible.
$35.00 – $40.00
Hippo: Marked:
"California USA C J 13"
$30.00 – $35.00

Camel: Marked: "J 8"
$55.00 – $60.00
Cow Jumping Over the Moon:
Unmarked:
$200.00 – $225.00

Lady Fish: Marked: "(c)
J 9 USA"
$30.00 – $35.00
Pinocchio Bust: Marked:
"C J 46 (c) USA"
$175.00 – $200.00

Turtle: Marked: "C J 14"
$30.00 – $35.00
Lady Fish: (Different color)
Marked: "(c) J 9 Calif USA"
Note! This fish has "Calif"
added to mark.
$30.00 – $35.00

Owl with Book: Marked: "J 4 USA"
$38.00 – $42.00
Mother Goose: Marked: "C J 16
USA"
$135.00 – $150.00

Cookie Cola: Marked: "C J 67
USA"
$50.00 – $55.00
Ketchup Bottle: Marked: "C J 68
USA"
$45.00 – $50.00

Slot Machine: Marked: "J 69
USA"
$45.00 – $50.00
Little Girl with Doll and Cookie:
Marked: "J-51 Calif."
$90.00 – $100.00

Milk Carton: Unmarked:
$40.00 – $45.00
Oreo Cookie: Unmarked:
$35.00 – $45.00

Elephant: Marked: "Calif
USA C J 15"
$40.00 – $45.00
Bear: Marked: "J 7 USA"
$42.00 – $48.00

Doranne of California

Rocking Horse: Marked: "USA J 63"
$42.00 – $46.00
Soda: Unmarked:
$45.00 – $50.00

Cupcake: Unmarked:
$40.00 – $45.00
Sundae: Unmarked:
$40.00 – $45.00

Snowman: Marked: "J 52"
$150.00 – $175.00
Walrus: Unmarked:
$58.00 – $62.00

Humpty Dumpty:
Marked:
"(c) USA C J 47"
$75.00 – $85.00
Pumpkin: Unmarked:
$30.00 – $35.00

ESMOND INDUSTRIES

The company was located in New York City, but didn't manufacture any pottery. They did contract other companies to manufacture their products. Thus the reason the Puriton lid fits this jar is because the jar was made by the Puriton company.

Blue and White Pencil Line Striped Jar: Marked:
"Esmond USA"
Note! This jar was "lidless"
but the Purinton fits perfectly.
$50.00 – $65.00

F. & F. MOLD & DIE WORKS

The F. & F. Mold & Die Corporation was formed in October of 1949. The company was commissioned to manufacture the very popular Aunt Jemima plastic cookie jar & matching spice sets and other accessories for the Quaker Oats Company. The cookie jar came either with a brown face or a black face. The brown one is much harder to find. I have shown both colors here for comparison. F. & F. Mold & Die Corporation ceased operation in December of 1987. The company was located in Dayton, Ohio.

Ken-L Ration Pup: Marked: "F & F Mold & Die Works Dayton Ohio Made in USA" $100.00 – $110.00

Aunt Jemima: Marked: "F & F Mold & Die Works Dayton Ohio Made in USA" $400.00 – $425.00
Aunt Jemima: Marked: "F & F Mold & Die Works Dayton Ohio Made in USA" $375.00 – $410.00

FIVE BRIDGES, INC.

Five Bridges located was founded in 1974 by Peter H. Minot and David Blocker on a ranch in Marana, Arizona. It was located on a road with a cattleguard, a culvert and three bridges–thus the name "Five Bridges" came to be. The first building to be used for the company was leased in 1976. David Blocker left the company in either '83 or '84. Now Minot is acting president. The Five Bridges now specialize in custom-imprinting of their existing line of more than 60 pieces, and custom-fabrication (like the Pepperidge Farm jar) for corporate give-away programs. The Five Bridges, Inc. is now located in Tucson, Arizona.

Pepperidge Farm Cookie Sack: Unmarked:
$80.00 – $100.00
Oreo-Double Stuff: Unmarked:
$40.00 – $50.00

FREDRICKSBURG ART POTTERY COMPANY

A pottery company was built in 1910 in Fredricksburg, Ohio. The company changed owners many times and later was named the Fredricksburg Art Pottery Company, (or F.A.P. Co. as we collectors call it), under the ownership of John McClain and George Heisler. It became known as the Fredricksburg Art Pottery Company in 1939. The company shut down in 1948.

Bartender: Marked: "USA"
$85.00 – $100.00
Windmill with Green Trim: Marked: "F.A.P. Co."
$55.00 – $65.00

Brown Bear: Marked: "F.A.P.
Co."
$55.00 – $60.00
White Bear: Marked: "F.A.P. Co."
Note! The mark on both bears is
written backwards, but can be read
properly if held up to a mirror.
$55.00 – $60.00

GILNER POTTERY

Information on Gilner Potteries is a mystery to me as of now. I do know it was located somewhere in California, and according to Jack Chipman, it was located in Culver City. I have been unable to obtain any information as such. I do know it was in operation in the mid 1950's as I've had pieces of pottery marked as such.

Rooster: Marked:
"Gilner G 622"
$50.00 – $55.00
Squirrel on Stump:
Marked: "Gilner Potteries
Design Pat."
$42.00 – $46.00

Gingerbread Boy: Marked: "Gilner" $100.00 – $125.00
Mammy Head: Unmarked: $2,000.00 – $2,200.00

Rooster: Marked: "Gilner G 622" $50.00 – $55.00
Bear: Marked: "G 405" $55.00 – $60.00

GREAT AMERICAN HOUSEWARES

There is no information available on this company. It was probably a distributor in New York since it is marked New York. I believe this jar was sold through the J.C. Penney stores.

Transformer: Marked: "Manufactured by Great American Housewares, Inc. New York-New York 10003 (c) Hasbro Bradley, Inc." All rights reserved. Made in Portugal.
$115.00 – $140.00

GREEN PRODUCTS

No information available on this company at this time.

Clown: Marked: "Kooky Klown (c) by newhauser pat pending Green Products Cleveland, O."
$115.00 – $130.00

N. S. GUSTIN

Founded in 1941 by Nelson Sage Gustin, the company is still in business and deals mostly in domestic wares. It was also a distributor for Los Angeles Pottery until that firm was liquidated. Gustin also has possession of the Los Angeles Pottery molds and they are still making cookie jars. Some will be marked N.S. Gustin, some just "Gustin" while others are marked "Los Angeles Potteries." Other jars are not marked, with the exception of perhaps a little brush stroke on the bottom. I believe these to be Designer-Craft, which is associated with Gustin & Los Angeles Potteries. Design Craft changed its name to Los Angeles Pottery, and is owned by David Gustin, grandson of N.S. Gustin.

Fat Cat: Unmarked:
$42.00 – $48.00
Fat Cat: Unmarked:
$42.00 – $48.00

Mouse with Cookie: Unmarked:
$45.00 – $55.00
Girl Holding Ice Cream Bar:
Unmarked:
$80.00 – $85.00

Mouse with Cookie: Unmarked:
$45.00 – $55.00
Sleeping Cat: Unmarked:
$60.00 – $70.00

Granny with Rolling Pin:
Marked: "N.S. Gustin Co."
$95.00 – $100.00
Rabbit with Carrot: Unmarked:
$45.00 – $50.00

HAEGER POTTERIES, INC.

In 1871, David Haeger owned a brickyard in Dundee, Illinois. This brickyard was transformed into an art pottery plant in 1914, when Edmund Haeger, David's son took leadership of the plant. Still in business today, Haeger is the oldest pottery in America that has remained in the hands of the same family who founded it.

M & M Jar: Unmarked:
This was a promotional item in '84 or '85.
$130.00 – $150.00
Keebler Tree House: Unmarked:
Note! Check this jar with the Keebler House in the McCoy section. Ernie was made in the mold on this one, whereas he is a decal on the McCoy one.
$90.00 – $110.00

Tri-Colored Jar: Marked: "Haeger
USA (c)"
$20.00 – $25.00
Cookie Barrel: Marked:
"Royal Haeger R 1657 USA"
$18.00 – $22.00

HALL CHINA COMPANY ———————————

Hall China Company was originally founded in 1903 at East Liverpool, Ohio, by Robert Hall and his son Robert T. Hall. The eldest Hall passed away in 1904, and Robert T. took over. Robert T. Hall's son John, has kept the pottery in operation and it's still in business today.

All the cookie jars shown in the Hall section were designed by Eva Ziesel. They also have the same mark which is–"Hall's Superior Quality Kitchen Ware Made in USA."

Dot: Marked as mentioned
above.
$65.00 – $75.00
Green Medallion: Marked as
mentioned.
$55.00 – $65.00

Golden Clover: Marked as mentioned.
$75.00 – $90.00
Basket: Marked as mentioned.
$55.00 – $65.00

French: Marked as mentioned.
$55.00 – $65.00

HARKER POTTERY COMPANY

Benjamin Harker, an English immigrant, came to East Liverpool, Ohio, and through much manual labor, such as hand-grinding his own clay, began Harker Pottery in 1840. In the '70's, the company reissued several of their Rockingham glaze pieces. Production of the Harker Pottery Company stopped after the sale of the company to the Jeanette Glass Company. What was once "The Oldest Pottery Company in America" dissolved in 1972.

Ruffled Tulip: Marked: "Hotoven
Harker
The Oldest Pottery in America
CHINAWARE"
$75.00 – $85.00

WM. H. HIRSCH MANUFACTURING COMPANY

I haven't been able to track down any information on this company. I was told in 1983 (by a former California ceramist) that Hirsch was only a distributor. However, Lois Lehner identifies them as being located in Hollywood, according to a 1946 Journal Directory. She also states seeing a "Los Angeles" mark.

Pinocchio: Marked: "Wm. H. Hirsch Mfg. Co.
L.A. Calif. USA (c) 60"
$175.00 – $200.00
Castle: Marked:
"Wm. H. Hirsch Mfg. Co. Calif. USA"
$150.00 – $175.00

Monk: Marked:
"Wm. H. Hirsch Mfg. Co.
L.A. Calif. USA (c) 58"
$50.00 – $55.00
Bee Hive: Marked: "W. Hirsch Mfg.
WH Made in USA"
$35.00 – $40.00

Old Fashioned Wall Phone: Marked:
Wm. H. Hirsch Mfg. Co."
$55.00 – $60.00
Cow: Marked: "Wm. H. Hirsch Mfg. Co."
$75.00 – $90.00

HOLIDAY DESIGNS, INC.

Located in Sebring, Ohio, Holiday Designs Incorporated began in 1964. The products have unusually bright colors to accommodate the modern kitchen. Their wares were distributed to firms such as Sears, Montgomery Ward, etc. Holiday Designs now operates as a part of Designer Accents, which was begun in early 1986. Holiday Design jars are not glazed on the bottom, as far as I know. This is the only way to differentiate between jars made by them and jars of the same mold by other companies.

Pumpkin: Unmarked:
$20.00 – $25.00
Wynken Blynken and Nod: Unmarked:
$35.00 – $38.00

Orange: Marked: "9045" $20.00 – $24.00
Bear: Marked: "USA" $30.00 – $35.00

Almost Home: Marked on the inside of jar: Almost Home 1986 Limited Edition of 20,000. 4832 "
$75.00 – $80.00
Pillsbury Doughboy: Marked: "The Pillsbury Company 1973"
Note! This jar is not glazed on the bottom! $72.00 – $78.00

Square Elephant: Marked:
"holiday designs u.s.a."
$60.00 – $65.00
Owl: Marked: "holiday designs u.s.a."
$35.00 – $38.00

Bear: Marked:
"u.s.a." on back of base, also
"(c) holiday designs" on rim of lid.
$45.00 – $50.00
King of Beasts: Marked:
"holiday designs u.s.a."
$38.00 – $42.00

Snoopy: Marked: "holiday designs"
on one leg "u.s.a." on other leg.
$50.00 – $55.00
Winking Face: Marked: "u.s.a."
$35.00 – $38.00

(a brown?) Snoopy: Marked:
"(c) holiday designs u.s.a."
$35.00 – $38.00
Dawg: Marked: "holiday designs
u.s.a."
$40.00 – $45.00

HOMER LAUGHLIN CHINA COMPANY

The Homer Laughlin China Company had its beginnings in East Liverpool, Ohio, in 1871. The company was started by Homer Laughlin and his brother. The brother withdrew and Homer continued on with the business. The business incorporated in 1886 and thereafter Homer Laughlin sold his interests in the company. Under new management, the company expanded and more plants were obtained. The growth of the business and different techniques being used required additional plants, and the company eventually moved to Newell, West Virginia, where they are located today.

Round Ball Shape with
Pastel Tulips: Marked:
"H L C Kitchen Kraft
Oven Serve USA"
$65.00 – $75.00
Round Ball Shape with
Colorful Tulips:
Marked: Same as Pastel
Tulip jar.
$65.00 – $75.00

HOUSE OF WEBSTER

The jars that we collectors have in our collections produced by House of Webster were not intended as such, but as containers for jams and jellies. The containers are made in Eastland, Texas, and are shipped to Rogers, Arkansas. The containers are filled in Rogers and then shipped to various places. As with cookie jars, many figural ones have been made.

Box of Strawberries:
Marked: "The House of
Webster Eastland Texas"
$15.00 – $18.00
Shock of Wheat:
Marked: "The House of
Webster Eastland Texas"
$16.00 – $18.00

HULL POTTERY COMPANY

The Hull Pottery Company began as the A.E. Hull Pottery, founded in 1905 by Addis E. Hull in Crooksville, Ohio. The company first manufactured stoneware, but later began making art pottery. In 1950, the plant was destroyed by a flood and a fire, but was rebuilt within two years and the company remained in business until 1986. Before the 1952 fire, the company used a capital "H" in their "Hull" wording, but began using the lowercase "h" after the company reopened.

Little Red Riding Hood:
Marked: "967 Hull Ware
Little Red Riding Hood
Patent Applied For USA"
$550.00 – $650.00
Little Red Riding Hood:
marked: "967 Hull Ware
Little Red Riding Hood
Patent Applied For USA"
$400.00 – $475.00

Little Red Riding Hood: Marked: "967 Hull Ware Little Red Riding Hood Patent Applied for USA"
$500.00 – $550.00
Little Red Riding Hood: Marked: "Little Red Riding Hood Pat. Des. 135889 USA"
Note! The cream colored L.R.R.H.'s have a glaze inside their heads,whereas the lids on the whiter ones are unglazed.
$500.00 – $550.00

Little Red Riding Hood:
Marked: "967 Hull Ware Little Red Riding Hood Patent Applied For"
$500.00 – $575.00
Little Red Riding Hood: Marked: "967 Hull Ware Little Red Riding Hood Patent Applied For USA"
$150.00 – $200.00

Little Red Riding Hood: Marked: "967 Hull Ware Little Red Riding Hood Patent Applied For USA"
$365.00 – $390.00
Barefoot Boy: (Unusual colors)
Unmarked except for the wording on the sides "Blessing on Thee Barefoot Boy"
$300.00 – $375.00

Crescent Jar: Marked:
"hull ovenproof USA B-8"
$35.00 – $40.00
Debonair Jar: Marked:
"hull ovenproof USA O-8"
$30.00 – $35.00

House and Garden Jar: Marked:
"hull ovenproof USA"
$28.00 – $30.00
Nuline Bak-Serve: Marked: "Hull
USA B-20"
$35.00 – $40.00

Gingerbread Boy: Marked:
"hull Crooksville Ohio
Ovenproof USA"
$55.00 – $65.00
Gingerbread Boy: Marked:
"hull Crooksville Ohio
Ovenproof USA"
$55.00 – $65.00

Heritageware: Marked: "hull USA
0-18"
$42.00 – $46.00
House and Garden: Marked:
"hull ovenproof USA"
$35.00 – $40.00

IMPERIAL PORCELAIN CORPORATION ——————

A pottery company was formed in Zanesville, Ohio, in 1946 by three doctors. It was sold in 1960 to a man named Denzil Harding who gave the company a name, which became known as Imperial Porcelain Corporation. The company produced a series of hillbillies or mountain folks which are very collectible today. The plant was destroyed by fire in 1967 and was never rebuilt.

Hillbilly: Marked: "USA", but know of
one marked "Zanesville Ohio"
$300.00 – $350.00
Daisy Mae: Marked: "USA" also
marked "Daisy Mae" on inner lid rim.
$400.00 – $450.00

LANE AND COMPANY

Lane and Company is yet another of the mystery companies we would like to know more about. According to marks on the jars we have, we know it existed in the 1950's. I have seen and have even had some of the lamps depicting the nursery rhyme tales, such as "Hey Diddle Diddle." They have been marked Van Nuys, California, but the cookie jars, and I know of only four at this time, are marked Los Angeles.

Sheriff: Marked: "(c) 1950 Lane & Co. Los Angeles Calif" $600.00 – $750.00
Indian Chief: Marked: "(c) 1950 (c) Lane & Co. Los Angeles Calif." $1,250.00 – $1,500.00

Clown with Umbrella: Marked: "Lane & Co. Los Angeles (c) 1950" $175.00 – $200.00
Churn: Marked: "Lane USA" $35.00 – $38.00

LOS ANGELES POTTERY

Los Angeles Pottery was in business from around 1940 until 1970, which was when the real estate was sold. After the premises were sold, N.S. Gustin received the better items for production at a plant of which he was already part owner. This plant was Design Craft and was located in West Los Angeles. The Los Angeles Pottery cookie jars were very popular, and one was produced in large quanities for the S. & H. Green Stamp Company. This one was the round barrel-like shape with different cookies (in relief) scattered around the jar and an English walnut for a finial on the lid.

Bakery: Marked: "(c) 1956 Made in USA Los Angeles Potteries XX95"
$40.00 – $45.00
Christmas Tree: Marked: "Los Angeles Potteries (c) 58 Made in USA XX99"
$35.00 – $40.00

Owl: Marked: "Los Angeles Pottery Calif USA #81 (c) 62"
$30.00 – $35.00
Woman with Striped Skirt: Marked: "Los Angeles Pottery (remainder illegible)"
$80.00 – $110.00

Gingerbread Men: Marked, but the glaze is so thick it's unreadable:
$40.00 – $50.00
Cookie Face: Marked: "Los Angeles Potteries Made in USA. XX96"
$50.00 – $55.00

Yellow Pear: Marked but unreadable:
$35.00 – $38.00
Yellow Apple: Unmarked:
Note! These jars also come in an avocado green
$30.00 – $35.00

Jar with Fruit: Marked: "Calif (c) USA"
$28.00 – $35.00
Pig: Marked: "Los Angeles Potteries Hand Decorated Calif USA"
$35.00 – $40.00

MADDUX OF CALIFORNIA

Maddux of California began operation in Los Angeles, California, in 1938. They were large makers and distributors of ceramic giftware. The last full year of manufacturing for Maddux was 1974. Maddux of California & Hollywood Ceramics (which was a subsidiary of Maddux) was sold in 1976.

Don't Let Go: (Little girl holding little boy's feet, while he's trying to reach an apple
Mark only partially readable: "M——Calif. (c) USA 2112"
$70.00 – $75.00
Chipmunk on Stump: Marked: "Maddux of Calif. (c) Romanell 2110"
$110.00 – $140.00

Shopping Cat: Marked: "(c) Maddux of Calif."
$125.00 – $150.00
Shopping Rabbit: Marked: "(c) Maddux of Calif."
$125.00 – $150.00

Queen: Marked: "Maddux of Calif. USA (c) 2104"
$115.00 – $140.00
King: Marked: "Maddux of Calif. USA (c) 2103"
$115.00 – $140.00

Baby Birds on
Bough: Marked:
"Maddux of Calif.
USA (c) 3233"
$40.00 – $50.00
Raggedy Andy:
Marked:
"Maddux of Calif.
USA (c) 2108"
$85.00 – $90.00

MARCIA CERAMICS OF CALIFORNIA ——————

Marcia Ceramics began as a family business in 1943. The business was owned and operated by George J. Siegel and his sons Gerald and Michael. Factories were set up in California, Arizona and Mexico. Plant #5 had 56,300 square feet and was set up at Sylmar, California. Items for Marcia were molded by Paulo Genduse. The company changed management in 1982.

Elephant: Marked: "(c) Calif. USA KJ11"
$40.00 – $45.00
Mushroom House: Unmarked:
$30.00 – $35.00

Bobby: Marked: "USA K04"
$40.00 – $50.00
Love Hippy: Unmarked:
$35.00 – $45.00

Snowman with Candy Cane: Marked:
"Marcia Ceramics (c) 84"
$90.00 – $100.00
Bear with Cookie: Marked:
"Marcia Ceramics (c) 84"
$35.00 – $40.00

Bear with Bee Hive On Stump: Unmarked:
$35.00 – $40.00
Playful Lion: Marked: "GK USA"
$40.00 – $45.00

Sheriff: Marked: "KJ 5 USA"
$40.00 – $45.00
Train: Unmarked:
$38.00 – $42.00

Tired Puppy: Marked: "USA GK 4" $40.00 – $45.00
Conductor Pig: Unmarked: $20.00 – $25.00

Tortoise and the Hare: Unmarked:
$25.00 – $30.00

MAURICE OF CALIFORNIA

This company was started in 1967 or perhaps a little prior to that. The company is still in operation.

Clown: Marked:
"1976 19(c)76 Pg 64 Maurice of Calif. USA"
$200.00 – $225.00

Basket of Fruit: Marked:
"Maurice Ceramics of
Calif. USA FR 211"
$25.00 – $30.00
Raggedy Ann: Marked:
"Maurice Ceramics
Calif. USA WD 33"
$60.00 – $70.00

Indian Scout: Marked: "Maurice of California" $45.00 – $50.00
Monkey: Marked: "Maurice of Calif. USA" $42.00 – $46.00

Chef Bust: Marked: "Maurice of Calif." $60.00 – $75.00
Shoe House: Marked, but glaze so thick, it is illegible: $40.00 – $45.00

METLOX POTTERIES

Metlox was founded by T.C. Proudy and his son Willis in 1927. The business made changes as to items they were manufacturing and also their locality. The elder Proudy passed away in 1931, but Willis continued making changes and the plant began producing dinnerware. In 1946 Proudy sold the company to Evan K. Shaw. Under this ownership, Metlox Potteries became a successful business. Kenneth Avery emerged as president of Metlox after the death of Evan Shaw. In 1988 Milinda Avery, daughter of Evan Shaw, became president and remained in that office until its closing in June of 1989. The Metlox cookie jars are highly collectible today. Many of the cookie jars Metlox manufactured were marked under their trade name, Poppytrail. Metlox Potteries were located in Manhattan Beach, California.

Little Red Riding Hood:
Marked: "Made in Poppytrail Calif. U.S.A."
$900.00 – $1,000.00
Cookie Girl:
Marked: "Made in Poppytrail Calif. USA"
$60.00 – $70.00

Shock of Wheat: Marked: "Made in Poppytrail Calif." $52.00 – $56.00
Blue Rooster: Marked: "Made in Poppytrail Calif." $120.00 – $135.00

Humpty Dumpty: Unmarked:
$325.00 – $375.00
Beau Bear: Marked:"Metlox
Calif. USA"
$45.00 – $55.00

Acorn with Woodpecker:
Unmarked:
$200.00 – $275.00
Acorn with Speckled Breasted
Woodpecker: Unmarked:
$240.00 – $290.00

Terra Cotta Lady: Marked: "Metlox
Calif. USA
(c) 87 by Vincient"
$300.00 – $350.00
Purple Cow with Butterfly: Marked:
"Made in Poppytrail Calif."
$350.00 – $400.00

Bundle of Corn:Marked:
"Made in Poppytrail Calif."
$55.00 – $60.00
Yellow Cow with Butterfly:
Marked:
"Made in Poppytrail Calif."
$350.00 – $400.00

Basset Hound: Marked:
"Metlox Calif. USA"
$350.00 – $400.00
Parrot: Marked: "Made in
Poppytrail Calif. USA"
$200.00 – $225.00

Sir Francis Drake: Marked:
"Made in Poppytrail Calif." USA"
$90.00 – $110.00
Slenderella Pig: Marked: "Metlox
Calif. USA"
$125.00 – $150.00

Calf Head: (Sometimes
mistaken for Elsie)
Unmarked:
$225.00 – $250.00
Clown Bust: Unmarked:
$90.00 – $110.00

Blue Bird on Stump:
Marked: "Made in USA"
$130.00 – $150.00
Lion: Marked:
"Made in Poppytrail Calif."
$160.00 – $170.00

Uncle Sam Bear: Marked:
"Metlox Calif USA"
$600.00 – $750.00
Pancho: Marked:
"Metlox Calif USA"
$70.00 – $75.00

Koala Bear: Marked: "Metlox Calif USA"
$115.00 – $135.00
Frosty Penguin: Marked: "Metlox Calif. USA"
$75.00 – $85.00

Bird on Pinecone: Marked:
"Made in USA"
$75.00 – $80.00
Flamingo: Marked:
"Metlox Calif USA"
$300.00 – $325.00

Katy Cat: Marked: "Metlox Calif. USA"
$75.00 – $85.00
Pierre: Marked: "Metlox Calif. USA"
$85.00 – $95.00

Puddles: Marked:
"Metlox Made in USA"
$100.00 – $115.00
Fish: Marked: "Pescado By
Metlox California Pottery
Manhatten Beach
Est. 1927"
$90.00 – $100.00

Rabbit on Cabbage:
Unmarked: (This jar in
production since 1957)
$150.00 – $175.00
Clown: Marked:
"Metlox Calif USA"
$125.00 – $150.00

Humpty Dumpty: Marked:
"Metlox Calif USA"
$125.00 – $140.00
Yellow Tulip: Marked:
"Made in USA"
$310.00 – $340.00

Cluster of Grapes:
Marked: "Made in USA"
(Also has two stickers)
$140.00 – $175.00
Apple: Marked:
"Made in USA"
$45.00 – $55.00

Snow Owl: Marked:
"Made in Poppytrail Calif."
$60.00 – $65.00
Blue/White Owl: Marked: "Made
in Poppytrail Calif"
$70.00 – $80.00

Pinocchio: Marked: "Made
in Poppytrail Calif. USA"
$275.00 – $300.00
Santa: Marked:
"Metlox Calif USA"
(Also has label as shown)
$250.00 – $275.00

Wally Walrus: Marked:"Made
in Poppytrail Calif USA"
$225.00 – $240.00
Blue Whale: Marked: "Made
in Poppytrail Calif USA"
$230.00 – $250.00

Twin Boy Head: Unmarked:
$250.00 – $275.00
Twin Girl Head: Unmarked:
$250.00 – $275.00

Topsy: (Two colors on apron)
Marked: "Metlox Calif USA"
$350.00 – $400.00
Roller Bear: Marked:
"Metlox USA"
$130.00 – $150.00

Black Santa: Marked:
"Original California Pottery" (Stamped)
also incised "Metlox Calif"
$410.00 – $425.00
Clown: Marked: "Made in Poppytrail Calif."
$125.00 – $150.00

Topsy in Yellow: Marked:
"Metlox Calif USA"
$330.00 – $350.00
Mammy in Yellow:
Marked: "Metlox Calif
USA" by Vincient:
$375.00 – $400.00

Topsy in Blue: Marked:
"Metlox Calif. USA"
$330.00 – $350.00
Mammy in Blue: Marked: "Original
California Pottery by Metlox"
$375.00 – $400.00

Topsy in Red: Marked: "Metlox
Calif USA"
$350.00 – $400.00
Mammy in Red: Marked:
"Metlox Calif USA"
Note! Next to the last time we
had talked to Metlox Potteries
they had told us they were trying
to get a redder red for the
Mammie's clothes. It's a shame it
couldn't have been. Their pottery
was a good quality.
$425.00 – $450.00

Panda Bear: Marked: "Metlox
Made in USA"
$75.00 – $85.00
Cookie Girl: Marked: "Made in
Poppytrail Calif. USA"
$80.00 – $100.00

Small Size Owl: Marked:
"Made in Poppytrail Calif"
$42.00 – $48.00
Owl: Marked:
"Made in Poppytrail Calif"
$40.00 – $45.00

Daisy Topiary Jar: Unmarked:
$65.00 – $75.00
Salty Pelican: Marked:
"Metlox Calif. USA"
$75.00 – $85.00

Dutch Girl with Mixing Bowl:
Marked: "Metlox Calif USA"
Note! This Dutch Girl base is
molded exactly like the
mammies (on pages 102, 103).
$170.00 – $190.00
Dutch Boy Grasping Suspenders:
Marked: "Metlox Calif USA"
$170.00 – $190.00

Dina: Marked: "Metlox Calif
USA by Vincient"
$130.00 – $145.00
Ballerina Bear: Marked:
"Metlox Calif. USA"
$115.00 – $140.00

Gingham Dog: Marked: "Made in Poppytrail Calif USA"
$135.00 – $150.00
Calico Cat: Marked: "Made in Poppytrail Calif USA"
$135.00 – $150.00

Lamb with Flower Necklace: "Made in Poppytrail Calif"
$190.00 – $215.00
Brownie (Younger Girl Scout): Unmarked except for sticker which reads "Metlox Manufacturing Company."
Metlox also made a Tiger Cub (Boy Scout) head that would be the same value as the Brownie.
$400.00 – $450.00

MORTON POTTERY COMPANY

Morton Pottery was founded by members of the Rapp family in Morton, Illinois, in 1922. Ronald Cowan and William York bought the pottery in 1969, but filed for bankruptcy in 1971. Somehow, the pottery was sold to AFK industries then sold to the Rival Manufacturing Company in Kansas City, Missouri, in 1972. The Rival Manufacturing Company is a maker of small kitchen appliances, which includes crock pots. The "crocks" for the crock pots were manufactured there. The pottery closed in 1979.

Basket of Fruit: Marked: "USA 3720"
$34.00 – $38.00
Green Hen with Chick on Back: Unmarked:
$55.00 – $60.00

Basket of Fruit: Marked: "USA-3720"
$34.00 – $38.00
Panda: Unmarked:
$65.00 – $75.00

Pineapple: Marked: "USA-3719" $25.00 – $30.00
Cookie Pot: Marked: "USA 3721" $30.00 – $35.00

Clown Face: Unmarked: $45.00 – $50.00
Clown Face: Unmarked: $45.00 – $50.00

MOSAIC TILE COMPANY

The Mosiac Tile Company was founded at Zanesville, Ohio, in 1894. When the company was first organized it had employed 30 people, but 31 years later its personnel was 1250. The one and only cookie jar that is known to have been manufactured by the Mosaic Tile Company was produced in the early 1940's. The company closed in 1967 because they couldn't compete with the cheap prices of foreign products coming to the United States.

Mammy with Pale Yellow Dress: Unmarked: $650.00 – $750.00
Mammy with Grayish-Blue Dress: Unmarked: $650.00 – $750.00

NELSON MCCOY POTTERY

The McCoy Pottery had its first beginnings in Putnam, Ohio, in 1848, but the cookie jars we collect today are attributed to the Nelson McCoy Pottery which originated in Roseville, Ohio, in 1910 by Nelson McCoy. After Nelson McCoy's death in 1945, Nelson Melick McCoy, a nephew of Nelson McCoy, became president. At the early age of 29, Nelson McCoy, Jr. stepped into the presidential shoes in 1954. In 1967, the pottery was sold to David T. Chase and Chase Enterprises. This firm also owned the Mount Clemens Pottery.

Mr. Chase sold his interests in the company to Lancaster Colony in 1974. The company was again sold in 1986 to citizens in New Jersey. In 1991 it was owned by Designer Accents of Sebering, Ohio, but was still known as Nelson McCoy ceramics. After years and years of pottery making and different ownerships, the McCoy Pottery ceased to exist.

Ball Shape with Ears:
Unmarked:
$26.00 – $30.00
Ball Shape with ears:
Unmarked:
$26.00 – $35.00

Cookie Pitcher: (Could be used for a water pitcher)
Unmarked:
$40.00 – $50.00
Cookie Pitcher: Unmarked:
$40.00 – $50.00

Bean Pot Type:
Unmarked:
$25.00 – $30.00
Bean Pot Type:
Unmarked:
$25.00 – $30.00

Yellow Milk Can with Ears:
Unmarked:
$35.00 – $40.00
Black Milk Can with Flowers:
Unmarked:
$35.00 – $40.00

Black with Flowers:
Unmarked:
$35.00 – $40.00
Peanut: Marked:
"260 McCoy USA"
$35.00 – $40.00

Milk Can with Poppies: Unmarked: $35.00 – $45.00
Milk Can with Star Shaped Flowers: Unmarked: $45.00 – $48.00

Cookie Jug Marked: "213 McCoy" $25.00 – $28.00
Cookie Jug: Unmarked: $26.00 – $30.00

Brown Cookie Jug: Unmarked: $15.00 – $18.00
Green Cookie Jug: Unmarked: $15.00 – $18.00

Cookie Jug–Rope Bottom: Marked:
"McCoy USA"
$25.00 – $30.00
Hillbilly Cookie Jug: Unmarked:
$24.00 – $28.00

Bicentennial Milk Can:
Marked: "McCoy 154 USA"
$38.00 – $42.00
Bicentennial Milk Can: Marked: "7019
USA McCoy"
$30.00 – $35.00
These milk cans are pictured this way to
show the reverse sides of both.

Modern Jar with Decals: Marked: "254
McCoy USA"
$25.00 – $30.00
Smiley Face: Marked: "McCoy USA"
$30.00 – $35.00

Pewter Look Tea Pot:
Marked: "McCoy USA"
$45.00 – $48.00
Copper Tea Pot:
Marked: "McCoy USA"
$45.00 – $50.00

Tea Kettle with Flowers
(Hammered Look):
Marked: "McCoy USA"
$35.00 – $40.00
Kookie Kettle: Marked:
"McCoy USA"
$25.00 – $30.00

Tea Kettle (Hammered
Copper look): Marked:
"McCoy USA"
$48.00 – $52.00
Nibble Kettle: Marked:
"McCoy USA"
This kettle was made with
different wording as shown
above.
$25.00 – $30.00

Nibble Kettle Bean Pot:
Marked: "McCoy USA"
$25.00 – $30.00
Aladdin Lamp
Style Tea Kettle:
(Hammered Look) Marked:
"McCoy USA"
Have seen this jar with
spring bail like one shown
beside this.
$50.00 – $55.00

Aqua Cookie Boy: Marked: "McCoy"
$140.00 – $160.00
Grandma with Gold Rimmed Glasses:
Marked: "159 USA"
$120.00 – $130.00

School Bus: Marked: "352 USA"
$35.00 – $40.00
Traffic Light: Marked: "351 USA"
$42.00 – $48.00

Wishing Well: **Note!** Color & gold trim:
Marked: "McCoy USA"
$150.00 – $175.00
Jar with Strawberries: Marked: "1123
USA"
$20.00 – $25.00

Cookie Tug: Marked: "354 USA"
$32.00 – $35.00
Clown in Barrel: Marked:
"McCoy USA"
$115.00 – $125.00

Red Bear: (I only know of two bears in
this color) Marked: "McCoy"
$200.00 – $250.00
Silver Grandfather Clock: Marked: "USA"
$150.00 – $175.00

Betsy Baker: (Much harder to find than Bobby) Marked: "184 McCoy USA"
$275.00 – $300.00
Heart Shaped Hobnail: Unmarked:
$375.00 – $425.00
Note the similarity as far as shape to the kissing penguins in my first book.

Western Grub Box: Marked:
"938 McCoy USA"
$40.00 – $50.00
Cookie Pot: Marked:
"McCoy USA"
$40.00 – $45.00

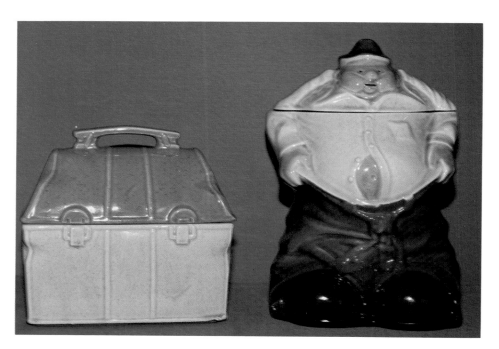

Lunch Bucket: Marked:
"357 USA"
$35.00 – $40.00
Chairman of the Board:
Marked: "162 USA"
$500.00 – $575.00

Coca-Cola Jug:
Marked: "1004 USA"
$55.00 – $65.00
Ice Cream Cone:
Marked: "159 USA"
$35.00 – $38.00

Winking Pig: Marked:"150 USA"
$230.00 – $250.00
Bubbles Cookie/Bank: Marked:
"224 USA"
$75.00 – $90.00

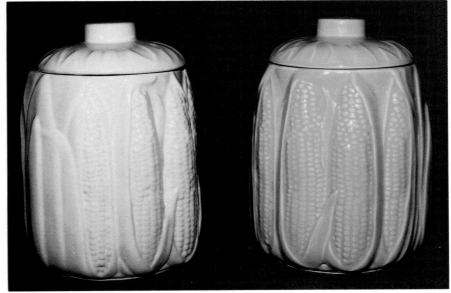

Ears of Corn: Marked:
"275 McCoy USA"
$48.00 – $52.00
Ears of Corn: Marked:
"275 McCoy USA"
$45.00 – $55.00

Dog House with Pink Bird
Finial: Unmarked:
$190.00 – $210.00
Thinking Puppy:
Marked: "0272 USA"
$30.00 – $35.00

Red Barn: Marked:
"McCoy USA"
$340.00 – $375.00
Keebler Tree House:
Marked: "350 USA"
$45.00 – $55.00
Compare this Keebler tree
house to the Haeger one!

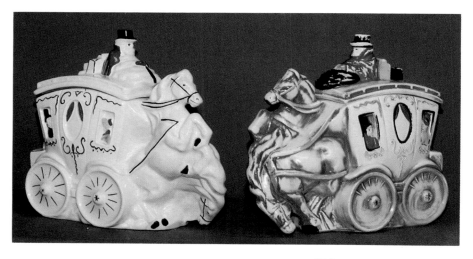

White Stage Coach with Gold
Trim: Unmarked:
$1,200.00 – $1,400.00
Cream/Brown Stage Coach:
Unmarked:
$1,400.00 – $1,600.00

Pirate's Chest: Marked: "252
McCoy USA"
$95.00 – $105.00
Buccaneer Jar: Unmarked:
$70.00 – $75.00

Hot Air Balloon: Marked:
"353 USA"
$38.00 – $42.00
Pagoda: Marked: "208-L
McCoy USA"
$25.00 – $30.00

Owl: Marked: "219 McCoy
USA"
$25.00 – $30.00
Woodsy Owl in Green:
Marked: "usa"
$275.00 – $325.00

Chilly Willy: Marked: "155 USA"
$40.00 – $45.00
Santa Cookie/Bank: Marked: "McCoy Limited"
$200.00 – $250.00

Gray Hocus: Marked: "211 McCoy USA"
$55.00 –- $65.00
Frog on Stump: Marked: "216 McCoy USA"
$55.00 –- $65.00

Little Boy Blue: Unmarked:
$70.00 – $80.00
Baa Baa Black Sheep: Unmarked:
$70.00 – $80.00
These two nursery rhyme jars
complete the series of six (6). The
other four are shown in my first
book on pages 93 & 94.

Sleeping Bear Surrounding
Bee Hive: Marked:
"143 USA"
$42.00 – $48.00
Elephant with Split Trunk:
Marked: "McCoy"
$475.00 – $500.00

Uncle Sam's Hat:
Marked: "USA"
$650.00 – $725.00
White Delicious Apple:
Marked: "McCoy 261 USA"
$28.00 – $32.00

Cat on Coal Bucket: Marked:
"218 USA"
$210.00 – $235.00
Girl Jumping Rope: Marked:
"McCoy USA"
$50.00 – $55.00

Spirit of 76: Marked: "9 USA"
(Incised) Also stamped "Carved
Wooden Eagle Artist unknown.
National Gallery of Art
Washington D.C."
$42.00 – $46.00
Milk Can with Gingham Flowers:
Marked: "333 McCoy USA"
$35.00 – $40.00

Freddy Gleep:
Marked: "McCoy USA"
$550.00 – $650.00
Bicentennial Milk Can:
Marked: "USA"
$28.00 – $32.00

Aqua Mammy: Marked:
"McCoy USA"
$800.00 – $900.00
Yellow Mammy: Marked:
"McCoy USA"
$800.00 – $900.00

White Turkey:
Marked: "McCoy"
$340.00 – $365.00
Green Turkey: Marked:
"McCoy"
$290.00 – $325.00
Compare these turkeys with the multicolored one in my first book. You will notice the tail feathers stand up straighter, but are not as flared.

Canister Type: Marked: "7024 USA"
$25.00 – $30.00
Train Engine: Marked: "McCoy USA"
$190.00 – $210.00

Flower Pot: Marked: "McCoy USA"
$210.00 – $235.00
Flower Pot: Marked: "McCoy USA"
$210.00 – $235.00

Cookie Bell: Unmarked:
$35.00 – $38.00
Bean Pot: (Considered a cookie jar by most collectors)
Marked: "McCoy"
$45.00 – $50.00

NORTH AMERICAN CERAMICS

Nite-Time Bear:
Unmarked:
$32.00 – $36.00
Woody Wagon: Marked:
"Acc J-6 (c) 1986 USA"
$130.00 – $160.00

Pink '57 Caddy: Marked:
"Acc J 3 (c) 1986 N.A.C. USA"
$130.00 – $160.00
Black 1950 Jaguar: Marked:
"Acc J 5 (c) 1986 N.A.C."
$125.00 – $150.00

Green '57 Chevy: Marked: "Acc J 4 (c) 1986 N.A.C. USA"
$130.00 – $160.00
Black Mercedes: Marked: "Acc J (c) 1986 N.A.C. USA"
$110.00 – $130.00

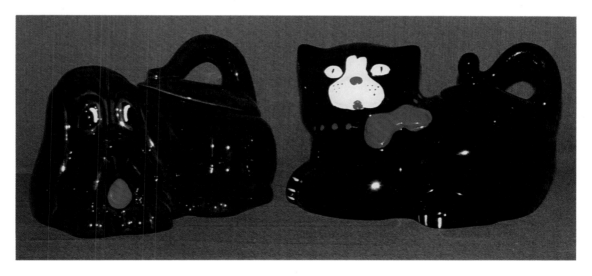

Basset Hound: Unmarked:
$35.00 – $40.00
Cat: Unmarked:
$28.00 – $34.00

NATIONAL SILVER COMPANY

The National Silver Company was another distributor that did not manufacture any of the products they sold. It is difficult to tell who made the cookie jars for them since they had several different companies commissioned to manufacture the items they sold.

Mammy: Marked: "N.S. Co." $275.00 – $300.00
Chef: Marked: "N.S. Co." $240.00 – $275.00

PETER PAN PRODUCTS, INC.

Information on this company is kind of sketchy. I believe it was a subsidiary of a distribution outlet used by the William Boyd Company of Beverly Hills, California. I once saw the cookie jar shown below (Hopalong Cassidy) with a small (probably 2x2) paper inside which read, "Peter Pan Products, Inc. William Boyd 1950."

Mr. Holly: Unmarked: $475.00 – $525.00
Hopalong Cassidy: (Bean Pot Style) Unmarked: $500.00 – $550.00

POTTERY GUILD INC.

Pottery Guild was a sales organization located in New York, which was started in 1937 by Mr. J. L. Block. In 1946, the organization expired.

Dutch Girl: Unmarked:
$55.00 – $65.00
Dutch Boy: Unmarked:
$55.00 – $65.00
These jars also come in solid blue and cream or light yellow as well as decorated.

Balloon Lady: Unmarked:
$150.00 – $165.00
Girl Holding Chest: Marked:
"Hand Painted Pottery
Guild of America"
$70.00 – $90.00

PURINTON POTTERY COMPANY

Purinton Pottery was started in 1936 at Wellsville, Ohio, by Bernard Purinton. The company moved to Shippenville, Pennsylvania, in 1941. They continued production until 1959 when the company closed for economic purposes.

Humpty Dumpy: Unmarked:
$475.00 – $525.00
Pear Design with Wooden Lid:
Unmarked:
$75.00 – $80.00

Two Fruit Design with Wooden Lid:
Unmarked:
$80.00 – $90.00
Rooster: Marked: "Purinton Slip
Ware"
$425.00 – $475.00
The Purinton rooster is the same mold as the Pottery Guild rooster in my first book. The Pottery Guild rooster is a brighter white and lighter weight.

Howdy Doody: Unmarked:
$675.00 – $725.00
Apple Design: Marked: "Purinton Slip Ware"
$80.00 – $85.00

Normandy Plaid: Unmarked:
$65.00 – $70.00

RANDSBURG COMPANY

The Harper Randsburg Company was another distributing company. It began operation in Toledo, Ohio, in 1908, but relocated in Indianapolis, Indiana, in 1912. The company not only sold pottery items, but also other items. Many of the cookie tins are marked with the Randsburg name on the paint palette and two brushes, which is their logo. Although many collectors do not care for these jars, if in perfect condition, I feel they are an asset to one's collection.

Asters: Marked: "Randsburg Genuine
Hand Painted Indianapolis USA"
$35.00 – $38.00

RED WING STONEWARE & POTTERIES

The Red Wing Stoneware Company was organized in Red Wing, Minnesota, in 1878. After merging with the Minnesota Stoneware Company, it became known as the Red Wing Union Stoneware Company in 1883. In 1920 the company began to make pottery and in 1936, the name was changed to Red Wing Potteries, Inc. By 1947, the production of all stoneware was discontinued, but the company continued to make pottery until its closing in 1967 because of a labor dispute.

Cattails (On Salt Glazed
Stoneware): Marked: "Red Wing
Art Pottery"
$200.00 – $225.00
Floral Jar: Unmarked:
$95.00 – $105.00

Floral Convex Jar with Rings:
Unmarked:
$42.00 – $48.00
Floral Crockery: Marked:
"Red Wing Saffron Ware"
$55.00 – $65.00

Floral Convex Jar with Rings:
Marked: "Red Wing Saffron
Ware"
$65.00 – $90.00
Jar with Poem–Happy the
Children: Unmarked:
$45.00 – $55.00

Pierre-Baker: Marked: "Red Wing
USA"
$210.00 – $225.00
Dutch Girl: (Katrina) Marked:
"Red Wing USA"
$225.00 – $250.00

King of Tarts: Marked: "Red
Wing USA"
$350.00 – $375.00
Queen of Tarts: Marked: "Red
Wing USA"
$510.00 – $550.00

Monk: Marked: "Red Wing
Pottery Hand Painted Pat D
130-328, D 130-329, D
130-330"
$60.00 – $65.00
Monk: Marked: "Red Wing
USA"
$165.00 – $190.00

Pineapple: Marked: "Red Wing"
$90.00 – $100.00
Rooster: Marked: "Red Wing
USA 249"
$75.00 – $90.00

Bunch of Bananas: Marked:
"Red Wing USA"
$65.00 – $75.00
Pear: Marked: "Red Wing USA"
$70.00 – $80.00

REGAL CHINA CORPORATION

The Regal China Corporation began in 1938. In 1955, they started producing the Trophy china decanters for Jim Beam. During and immediately following World War II, the company produced items such as salt and pepper shakers, canister sets, cookie jars, and vases for Marshall Field and other retailers. All the products manufactured at their plant were porcelain. The company closed in June of 1992.

Cat: (White) Unmarked:
$375.00 – $400.00
Fifi, the French Poodle: Marked:
"Fifi (c) C. Miller 1163"
$525.00 – $575.00

Dutch Girl: Unmarked:
$375.00 – $425.00
Dutch Girl: Unmarked:
$375.00 – $425.00

Little Red Riding Hood: White with Gold:
Marked: "Little Red Riding Hood Pat-Des
135889 USA"
Note! This jar is HULL, but shown here with
Regal Goldilocks.
$300.00 – $375.00
Goldilocks: Marked: "405"
$250.00 – $275.00

Kraft T. Bear: Marked: "Genuine Regal
China, Made in USA, Kraft, Inc." T. Bear has
signed his name "T. Bear" inside his mark
(Paw Print)
$175.00 – $200.00
Hubert: Marked: "Hubert, made in USA"
This jar given away as a premium at a Chicago
bank.
$475.00 – $525.00

Peek-A-Boo: Marked: "Peek-A-Boo Van Telligen (c)" $1,400.00 – $1,575.00
Tulip Jar: Unmarked: $65.00 – $75.00

The Three Bears: Marked: "The Three Bears 704" $200.00 – $225.00
Toby Cookies: Unmarked: $575.00 – $625.00

ROBINSON RANSBOTTOM POTTERY COMPANY —

Charles, Ed, Frank and Mort, all members of the Randsburg family, founded the pottery in 1900. The company, located in Roseville, Ohio, is still in operation today. This company is sometimes confused with the Roseville Pottery Company of Zanesville, Ohio, simply because of the "Roseville" which is part of their mark.

Ole King Cole: Marked:
"R.R.P. Co. Roseville,
O USA"
$400.00 – $425.00
Tiger Cubs: Marked:
"R.R.P. Co. Roseville,
Ohio 386"
$50.00 – $60.00

World War II Soldier-Bud:
Unmarked:
$150.00 – $165.00
World War II Sailor-Jack:
Unmarked:
$150.00 – $165.00

Dutch Girl: Marked: "R.R.P. Co. Roseville Ohio No.—"
$125.00 – $135.00
Dutch Boy: Marked: "R.R.P. Co. Roseville Ohio No. 423"
$125.00 – $135.00

Whale: Marked:
"R.R.P. Co. Roseville O USA"
$975.00 – $1,050.00
Chef with Bowl & Spoon:
Gold Trim: Marked:
"R.R.P. Co. Roseville Ohio 411"
$180.00 – $200.00

Dutch Girl with Gold Trim: Marked:
"R.R.P. Co. Roseville Ohio No.—"
$250.00 – $275.00
Dutch Boy with Gold Trim: Marked:
"R.R.P. Co. Roseville Ohio No. 423"
$250.00 – $275.00

ROMAN CERAMICS

Located in Mayfield, Kentucky, this company was in business from 1972 until 1988.

R2D2: Marked: "Star Wars TM (c) 1977 Twentieth Century-Fox Film Corporation" $165.00 – $175.00
CP30: Marked: "Star Wars TM (c)1977 Twentieth Century-Fox Film Corporation" $250.00 – $300.00
Note! I have seen an ice-bucket of R2D2, and the only way to differentiate between the two is the ice bucket has a plastic lining and a small hole in the bottom. The cookie jar does not!

ROSEVILLE POTTERY COMPANY

George Young founded the Roseville Pottery Company in Roseville, Ohio, in 1892. The company relocated in Zanesville, Ohio, in 1898. Although the company moved to Zanesville, the company kept the Roseville name until its closing in 1954.

Freesia: Marked: "Roseville USA 3-8" $250.00 – $275.00
Clematis: Marked: "Roseville USA 3-8" $210.00 – $230.00

SHAWNEE POTTERY COMPANY

The Shawnee Pottery Company had its beginnings in Zanesville, Ohio, in 1937. The company name "Shawnee" was decided upon after the discovery of an arrowhead, found by Malcolm Schweiker. The Pottery's earliest trademark was a Shawnee Indian with an arrowhead. Shawnee's first designer was a German named Rudy Ganz. He was with the company from 1939 to 1944. His cookie jar designs were very popular. Among them are the Smiley and Winnie Pigs, the Sailor Boy, also Jack and Jill, which we collectors have called Dutch Boy and Dutch Girl for much too long. I feel it's time we call them by their intended names. He also designed the Elephant, the Puss 'n' Boots Cat and probably the Muggsy. The company became very successful, but with the impact of foreign imports and their cheap prices, the company could not compete and closed in 1961.

Aqua Hexagon:
Marked: "USA"
$120.00 – $135.00
Blue Hexagon:
Marked: "USA"
$120.00 – $135.00

Drum Major:
Marked: "USA"
$245.00 – $265.00
Tulip Jug:
Marked: "USA 75"
$165.00 – $190.00

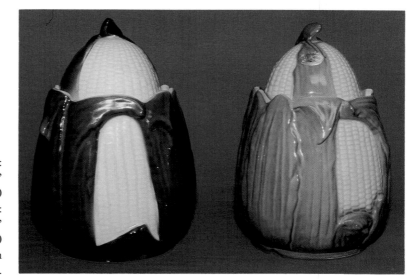

Corn Queen: Marked:
"Shawnee USA 66"
$190.00 – $215.00
Corn King: Marked:
"Shawnee USA 66"
$125.00 – $140.00
Note! The Queen is much lighter than
the King and is much harder to find.

Smiley Pig with Sweet Clover Bloom:
Marked: "Patented Smiley USA"
$225.00 – $275.00
Ball Shape with Starburst Design:
Marked: "USA"
$60.00 – $75.00

Winnie C. J. with Bank: Marked:
"Patented Winnie Shawnee USA 61"
$400.00 – $450.00
Smiley C.J. with Bank: Marked: "Patented
Smiley Shawnee USA 60"
$325.00 – $375.00

Shawnee Pottery Company

Baker & Gingerbread Boy:
Marked: "USA"
$135.00 – $155.00
Baker & Gingerbread Boy
with Gold Trim:
Marked: "USA"
$220.00 – $250.00

Dutch Boy:
Marked:
"Great Northern
USA 1025"
$325.00 – $350.00
Dutch Girl:
Marked:
"Great Northern
USA 1026"
$375.00 – $400.00
Note! Although
Great Northern
Pottery designed
their own jars, I
believe they copied
the Shawnee Jack &
Jill, but made it
smaller.

Basket of Fruit with Gold
Trim: Marked: "Shawnee
USA 84"
$200.00 – $225.00
Cooky: This is Jill with
gold trim. Since it was
decorated in gold, the
decorator added the
"Cooky" name in gold:
"USA"
$300.00 – $325.00

Clown with Seal: Gold trim--Note gold stars
on this jar. Marked: "Shawnee USA 12"
$775.00 – $815.00
Sailor with Gold Trim and Black Hair:
Marked: "USA"
$725.00 – $775.00

Cooky: "Gold Trim": (Again Jill)
Unmarked or glaze so heavy it doesn't show.
$275.00 – $300.00
Cooky: "Gold Trim": (Again Jill)
Marked: "USA"
$275.00 – $300.00

Cooky: Gold Trim: (Jill) Marked: "USA"
$300.00 – $325.00
Happy: Gold Trim: (Jack) Marked: "USA"
$280.00 – $310.00

Winnie Pig with Sweet Clover & Gold
Trim: Marked: "USA"
$425.00 – $450.00
Smiley Pig with Sweet Clover & Gold
Trim: Marked: "Patented Smiley USA"
$700.00 – $750.00

Smiley Pig with Gold Trim & Decals:
Marked: "USA"
$300.00 – $325.00
Smiley Pig with Gold Trim & Decals:
Marked: "USA"
$300.00 – $325.00

Winnie with Gold Trim:
Marked: "Patented Winnie USA"
$400.00 – $425.00
Smiley Pig with Rose Decals & Gold
Trim: Marked: "USA"
$425.00 – $450.00

Puss 'n' Boots with Flowers & Gold Trim:
Marked: "Patented Puss 'n' Boots USA"
$350.00 – $375.00
Muggsy with Flowers & Gold Trim:
Marked: "Patented Muggsy USA"
$800.00 – $875.00

House: Marked: "USA 6"
$825.00 – $875.00
Muggsy with Flowers & Gold
Trim: Marked: "Patented
Muggsy USA"
$750.00 – $800.00

Cooky with Flowers & Gold
Trim: Marked: "USA"
$300.00 – $325.00
Happy with Patches & Gold Trim:
Marked: "USA"
$275.00 – $300.00

SIERRA VISTA CERAMICS

Sierra Vista Ceramics started in 1942. The business began as a partnership owned by Reinhold Lenaburg and his son Leonard. Selling his interest in the business to Leonard, the father retired in 1951. Leonard relocated in Phoenix, Arizona.

Cookie House 7 Cookie Alley: (House has plastic window) Marked: "Sierra Vista Ceramics Pasadena Calif Made in USA"
$60.00 – $65.00
(Scared) Humpty Dumpty: (He's started to fall) Marked: Sierra Vista Ceramics (c) 57 Pasadena Cal. USA."
$135.00 – $155.00

Rooster with Ruffled Feathers: Marked: "Sierra Vista Ceramics Pasadena Calif USA (c) 1958"
$75.00 – $90.00
Rooster: Marked: "Sierra Vista California"
$60.00 – $65.00
This last rooster was shown in my first book, but is shown here for comparison.

Spaceship with Martians:
Marked: "Sierra Vista
Ceramics Pasadena Cal. (c)
57 USA"
$225.00 – $250.00
Tug Boat: Marked: "Sierra
Vista California"
$100.00 – $110.00

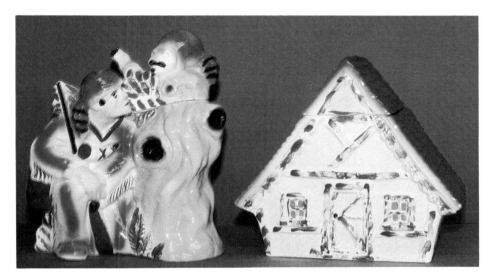

Davy Crockett: Marked:
"Sierra Vista of California
(C) 57"
$850.00 – $925.00
House (Reversible)
Marked: "Sierra Vista (c)
51 California"
$100.00 – $125.00

Gray Poodle: Marked: "Sierra
Vista of California (c)"
$125.00 – $150.00
House: Reverse side of house
shown above.

Circus Wagon Car: Marked: "Sierra Vista Ceramics Pasadena Cal (c) 1957 USA" $55.00 – $60.00
Sad Bear: Marked: "Sierra Vista 19 (c) 51 California" $50.00 – $55.00

House with High Pitched Roof: Marked: "Sierra Vista (c) 53 California USA" $70.00 – $75.00
Elephant: Marked: "Sierra Vista California" $75.00 – $85.00

Toadstools with Toad: Marked: "Sierra Vista Ceramics Pasadena Cal. USA (c) 1952" $45.00 – $50.00
Homecoming King: Unmarked: $300.00 – $325.00

STONEWARE DESIGNS WEST

Dunce Head: Unmarked:
$32.00 – $36.00
Woman: Unmarked:
This jar has man to match.
$38.00 – $45.00

STANFORD POTTERY INCORPORATED

The Stanford Pottery began operation in 1945 in Sebring, Ohio. In early 1961, the pottery (as with so many other pottery companies) was destroyed by fire and never rebuilt.

Pottery Design: Marked: "#520 B Stanford Sebring O. Made In USA"
$24.00 – $28.00
Plaid Design: Marked: "#__B Stanford Sebring O. Made in USA"
$24.00 – $28.00

White Tomato with Gold Trim: Unmarked: $35.00 – $40.00
Red Tomato: Marked: "The Pantry Parade Co. USA" $30.00 – $35.00

STARNES OF CALIFORNIA

I have no information on this company at present. However, Lois Lehner has listed a Walter Starnes in her book as being listed in the 1952 & 1954 Crockery and Glass Journal with a Los Angeles location. We presume this is the Starnes connected with Starnes of California and the Sierra Vista Company. While studying many cookie jars, I feel that the Starnes of California Company used more grays in their coloring than any other company. I also feel that the gray Whale in the unknown section of this book may indeed be a Starnes jar.

Cloth Doll: Unmarked: $85.00 – $95.00
Cloth Doll: Unmarked: $75.00 – $85.00

Noah's Ark: Marked:
"Pat-Pend Starnes of
Calif (c)"
$150.00 – $175.00
Pirate on Chest: Marked:
"Pat-Pend Starnes of
California (c)"
$300.00 – $325.00

Queen Bee on Bee Hive:
Unmarked:
$350.00 – $400.00
Bear on Blocks: Unmarked:
$80.00 – $90.00

Dennis the Menace: Unmarked:
$550.00 – $600.00
Little Girl: Unmarked:
$500.00 – $575.00

Old Fashioned Wall Phone:
Marked: "Pat. Des. 178703 (or
198703) Walter Starnes"
$65.00 – $70.00
Doghouse with Dog–Howling
Cat on Roof: Unmarked:
$125.00 – $135.00

TERRACE CERAMICS INC. ─────────

John Bonistall, former and last president of the Shawnee Pottery, bought the Shawnee molds when that company closed. He started a business in Marietta, Ohio, in 1963. In 1964, he relocated in Zanesville, Ohio. The company went out of business in 1975.

Muggsy Look-A-Like:
Marked: "Terrace Ceramics
USA 4254"
$75.00 – $85.00
Thumper Look-A-Like:
Marked: "Terrace Ceramics
USA 4253"
$50.00 – $55.00

Bean Pot Type with Horse & Stagecoach Scene: Marked: "Genuine Porcelain
Terrace Ceramics Zanesville Ohio. USA 6711"
$85.00 – $95.00

TREASURE CRAFT

Alfred Levin started the Treasure Craft Company in 1945. It was originally based in Gardena, but relocated to Compton. The company was sold to the Pfaltzgraff Company in 1988.

Trolly Car: Marked: "Treasure Craft Made in USA"
$38.00 – $42.00

Bull Dog Cafe: Marked:
"Treasure Craft Made in
USA (c) Disney"
$75.00 – $85.00
Mrs. Potts: Marked:
"Treasure Craft Made in
USA (c) Disney"
$65.00 – $75.00

Cookie Shack: Marked: "Treasure Craft
19(c)60 Compton Calif."
$40.00 – $45.00
Baseball Rabbit: Marked: "Treasure Craft
USA 19(c)68 Calif"
$40.00 – $48.00

Elephant Sailor: Marked:
"Treasure Craft (c) USA"
$40.00 – $45.00
Hobo Clown: Marked: "Treasure
Craft USA"
$50.00 – $55.00

Sugar with Button Eyes: Marked: "(c)
Treasure Craft USA"
$50.00 – $55.00
Spice with Button Eyes: Marked: "(c)
Treasure Craft USA"
$80.00 – 85.00

Santa with Glass Belly: Marked:
"Treasure Craft (c) Made In USA"
$90.00 – $100.00
Snowman with Glass Belly: Marked:
"Treasure Craft (c) Made in USA"
$90.00 – $100.00

Gumball Machine:
Marked: "Treasure Craft (c) Made
In USA"
$45.00 – $50.00
Monkey with Glass Belly:
Marked: "Treasure Craft (c) Made
in USA 454"
$70.00 – $80.00

Santa Fe Cafe: Marked: "(c)
Treasure Craft USA"
$45.00 – $55.00
Noah's Ark: Marked:
"Treasure Craft (c) Made in
USA"
$40.00 – $45.00

Cactus: Marked: "(c) Treasure Craft Made in USA"
$45.00 – $50.00
Western Boot with Pistol Finial: Marked: "Treasure Craft (c) Made in USA"
$50.00 – $55.00

Monkey: Marked: "Treasure Craft 1968 (c) Compton Calif."
$40.00 – $48.00
Owl: Marked: "Treasure Craft (c) Made in USA"
$55.00 – $60.00

English Bobby: Marked: "Treasure Craft (c) Made in USA"
$40.00 – $45.00
Hobo Clown: Marked: "Treasure Craft (c) Made in USA"
$40.00 – $45.00

Lamb: Marked: "Treasure
Craft 19(c)68 Calif"
$45.00 – $48.00
Cocker Spaniel: Unmarked:
$40.00 – $45.00

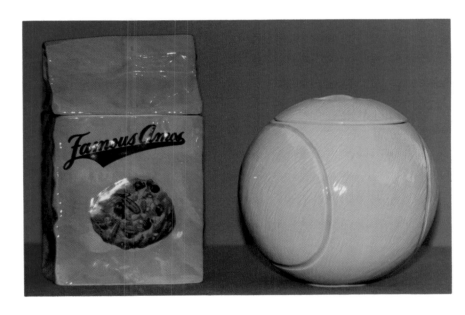

Cookie Sack: Marked:
"Treasure Craft (c) Made in
USA"
$50.00 – $55.00
Tennis Ball: Marked:
"Treasure Craft (c) Made in
USA"
$38.00 – $42.00

Puppy in Wooden Bucket: Marked:
"Treasure Craft (c) Made in USA"
$45.00 – $50.00
Cat with Mouse: Marked: "Treasure
Craft (c) Made in USA"
$38.00 – $42.00

Cat in Wooden Bucket:
Marked: "Treasure Craft
(c) Made in USA"
$45.00 – $50.00
Sheep Dog: Marked:
"Treasure Craft (c) Made in
USA"
$38.00 – $42.00

Rooster: Unmarked:
$40.00 – $45.00
Watering Can: Marked: "(c)
Treasure Craft USA"
$50.00 – $55.00

Sitting Clown: Marked: "Treasure
Craft (c) Made in USA"
$40.00 – $45.00
Cookie Chef: Marked: "Treasure
Craft (c) Made in USA"
$35.00 – $38.00

Ma's Cookie Books:
Marked: "Treasure Craft
(c) Made in USA"
$50.00 – $55.00
Grandma: Marked:
"Treasure Craft (c)
Made in USA"
$48.00 – $52.00

Angel: Marked: "Noel
(c) Treasure Craft USA"
$85.00 – $95.00
Grandma: Marked:
"Treasure Craft (c)
Made in USA"
$48.00 – $52.00

Carousel: Marked:
"Treasure Craft (c)
Made in USA"
$40.00 – $50.00
Old Radio: Marked:
"Treasure Craft (c)
Made in USA"
$40.00 – $45.00

Covered Wagon: Marked:
"Treasure Craft (c) USA"
$40.00 – $45.00
Train: Marked: "Treasure
Craft (c) USA"
$40.00 – $45.00

Cat Holding Rose: Marked:
"(c) Susan-Marie Treasure
Craft USA"
$40.00 – $45.00
Mouse: Marked: "(c)
Treasure Craft Made In
USA"
$30.00 – $35.00

Cookie Barn: Marked:
"Treasure Craft (c) USA"
$30.00 – $35.00
Elmer, the Learning Tree:
Marked:
"Treasure Craft (c) USA"
$110.00 – $125.00

Bandito: Marked:
"Treasure Craft (c) Made
in USA"
$58.00 – $62.00
Stagecoach: Marked:
"Treasure Craft (c) USA"
$50.00 – $55.00

Rocking Horse: Marked:
"Treasure Craft (c) Made
in USA"
$48.00 – $52.00
Cow: Marked: "Treasure
Craft (c) Made in USA"
$30.00 – $35.00

Stuffed Cat: Marked:
"Treasure Craft (c) Made
in USA"
$35.00 – $40.00
Kitten with Goldfish Bowl:
Marked: "Treasure Craft
(c) Made in USA"
$40.00 – $45.00

Big Al: Marked: "(c) Walt Disney Productions"
$115.00 – $130.00
Cookie Van: Marked: "Treasure Craft (c) Made in USA"
$60.00 – $70.00

Juke Box: Marked: "Treasure Craft (c) Made In USA"
$90.00 – $115.00
Pot Bellied Stove: Marked: "Treasure Craft (c) Made in USA"
$34.00 – $38.00

Seymour Snail: Marked: Lid marked: "Treasure Craft (c) Made in USA" Base is marked: "9(c) 1983 David Kirschner Productions All rights reserved"
$90.00 – $115.00
Golf Ball: Unmarked:
$38.00 – $48.00

Owl Graduate: Marked:
"Treasure Craft (c) Made in
USA"
$30.00 – $35.00
P. D. in Football House: Lid
is marked: "Treasure Craft (c)
Made in USA"
Base is marked: "(c) 1983
David Kirschner Productions
All rights reserved"
$75.00 – $90.00

Ice Wagon: Marked:
"Treasure Craft (c) USA"
$45.00 – $48.00
P. D. the Coach: Lid is
marked: "Treasure Craft (c)
USA" Base is marked: "David
Kirschner Productions All
rights reserved"
$100.00 – $125.00

Football: Marked: "Treasure
Craft Made in USA (c)"
$38.00 – $42.00
Baseball: Marked: "Treasure
Craft Made in USA (c)"
$38.00 – $42.00

Eight Ball: Marked: "Treasure Craft Made in USA (c)" $38.00 – $42.00
Porgo on Sled with Christmas Gift: Marked: "Treasure Craft Made in USA" and "Designed by David Straus
(c) 1987 Hallmark Cards" $65.00 – $75.00

Roly : Marked: "Treasure Craft (c) Disney" $65.00 – $75.00
Roly with Glass Treat Bowl: Marked: "(c) Treasure Craft Made in USA" $50.00 – $55.00

TWIN WINTON CERAMICS

The Twin Winton Ceramics originally started in 1936 after the Winton family moved to Pasadena, California, from Canada. The twin brothers, Ross and Don, were first in a partnership with Helen Burke who decorated and sold the wares. The business was then known as Burke-Winton. In 1939, the Wintons receded from the partnership and began their own business. In 1942, the brothers enlisted in the service and naturally their business was inactive. In 1946, the Twin Winton Ceramics was once again in full operation. In 1952, they sold their interest in the company to their older brother Bruce. Don Winton, working as a free lance, designed and molded the very popular cookie jars and accessories. In 1964, Twin Winton moved to San Juan Capistrano and continued business until the company was sold in 1975. After Bruce Winton retired, the molds were sold to the Treasure Craft Company of Compton, California. Ross Winton died in 1980 and Bruce in 1991. Don Winton is still active and in 1991 sculptured a three-times life size bronze bust of ex-president Ronald Reagan which was offered as a donation to the President's new library in Ventura County.

Cookie Bucket: Marked: "(c) Twin Winton (c) 59"
$40.00 – $45.00
Rooster: Marked: "Twin Winton (c) 59"
$50.00 – $55.00

Ole King Cole: (Blue Trim) Marked: "Twin Winton USA"
$220.00 – $240.00
Squirrel on Nut House: (Really a candy jar) Unmarked:
$32.00 – $36.00

Rooster with Very High Gloss: Marked: "Twin Winton (c) 59"
$60.00 – $70.00
Ole King Cole: (Yellow Trim) Marked: "Twin Winton (c) California USA"
$220.00 – $240.00

Duck with Mixing Bowl: "Twin Winton (c) Calif USA"
$70.00 – $75.00
Magilla? Gorilla: Marked: "Twin Winton (c) San Juan Capistrano Calif."
$330.00 – $365.00

Persian Kitten: Marked: "Twin Winton Calif. USA (c) 63"
$60.00 – $70.00
Cookie Time: Marked: "Twin Winton (c) 60 Made in USA"
$44.00 – $48.00

Chipmunk: Marked:
"Twin Winton (c) Calif USA"
$50.00 – $60.00
Modern Head: Marked:
"Twin Winton (c) Calif. USA"
$125.00 – $150.00

Lion: Marked:
"Twin Winton (c) Calif. USA"
$40.00 – $45.00
Bambi: Marked:
"Twin Winton (c) Calif. USA"
$70.00 – $80.00

Grandma: Marked:
"Twin Winton Calif. USA (c) 1962"
$80.00 – $90.00
Pot Bellied Stove: Unmarked:
$45.00 – $50.00

Cookie Barn: Marked: "Twin Winton (c) California USA"
$40.00 – $45.00
Cookie Barrel: Marked: "(c) The Twin Wintons"
$45.00 – $50.00
Note! There is another Twin Winton Cookie Barrel with mouse on lid and woman's head (possibly mammy) on front.

Butler: Marked: "Twin Winton (c) Calif USA"
$70.00 – $75.00
Cookie Churn: Marked: "Twin Winton (c) Calif. USA"
$60.00 – $70.00

Cookie Wagon: Unmarked: $90.00 – $100.00
Pumpkin Coach: Marked: "Twin Winton (c) California USA"
$85.00 – $95.00

Train: Marked: "Twin Winton (c) Calif USA" $45.00 – $50.00
Catcher: Marked: "Twin Winton (c) Made in USA" $75.00 – $80.00

Fire Engine: Marked: "Twin Winton (c) Calif. USA" $45.00 – $55.00
Cop: Marked: "Twin Winton (c) Calif USA" $65.00 – $70.00

Child in Shoe: Marked: "Twin Winton (c) Calif USA" $40.00 – $45.00
Donkey with Cart: Unmarked, probably had been stamped. $70.00 – $75.00

Bear: Unmarked:
$45.00 – $50.00
Cookie Nut: Marked: "Twin Winton (c)
Calif USA"
$45.00 – $50.00

Goose: Marked: "Twin Winton
1964 (c) California USA"
$65.00 – $70.00
Raccoon: Marked: "Twin
Winton (c) Calif USA"
$65.00 – $75.00

Cook Stove: Unmarked:
$85.00 – $90.00
Buddha: Marked: "Twin Winton (c) San
Juan Capistrano Calif. USA"
$55.00 – $60.00
This jar was stamped over a stamp or
double stamped.

Pot O' Cookies: Marked:
"Twin Winton San Juan
Capistrano Calif USA"
$30.00 – $35.00
Pot O' Cookies: Marked:
"Twin Winton San Juan
Capistrano Calif USA"
$40.00 – $45.00

Elf: Marked: "Twin Winton
(c) '63 Made in Calif USA"
$60.00 – $65.00
(candy jar not cookie)
Cookie TeePee: Marked:
"Twin Winton (c) Calif.
USA"
$130.00 – $150.00

Cookie Shack: Marked:
"Twin Winton (c) Calif
USA"
$45.00 – $50.00
Pirate Fox: Marked:
"Twin Winton Made in Calif
USA (c) 63"
$55.00 – $65.00

Cookie Shack: Marked: "Twin Winton (c) San Juan Capistrano Calif USA" $45.00 – $50.00
Cookie Shack: Marked: "Twin Winton (c) Calif USA" $45.00 – $50.00

Owl: Marked: "Twin Winton Collectors Series (c) California USA" $90.00 – $110.00
Frog: Marked: "Twin Winton (c) Santa Monica Calif" $75.00 – $80.00

Raggedy Andy: Marked: "Twin Winton Collector Series (c) USA"
Also, looks as if signed by decorator on rim of lid. Possibly LJL. $125.00 – $140.00
Raggedy Ann: Marked: "Twin Winton Collector Series (c) USA" $125.00 – $150.00

Cookie Elf: Marked: "Twin Winton (c)
San Juan Capistrano Calif. USA"
$90.00 – $115.00
Cookie Elf: Marked: "Twin Winton (c)
Calif USA"
$50.00 – $55.00

Donkey: Marked: "Twin Winton (c) Calif
USA" also stamped "Twin Winton (c)
Collectors Series California USA" This jar
too, looks as signed LJL.
$115.00 – $130.00
Donkey: Marked: "Twin Winton (c) Calif
USA"
$50.00 – $60.00

Police Chief Bear: Marked: "Twin Winton (c)
San Juan Capistrano Calif USA"
$110.00 – $120.00
Police Chief Bear: Marked: "Twin Winton (c)
San Juan Capistrano Calif. USA"
$50.00 – $55.00

Gun Slinger Rabbit: Marked: "Twin Winton Collectors Series California USA"
$120.00 – $130.00
Also "Twin Winton Calif USA (c)" then in red ink "YC"
Gun Slinger Rabbit: Marked: "Twin Winton Calif USA"
$65.00 – $70.00

VALLONA STARR

Vallona Starr was a trade name for Triangle Studios (such as Poppytrail was for Metlox) which was located in Los Angeles in '45 through '48 but located in El Monte, California, in 1949. In 1951, the Triangle Studio's name was changed to Vallona Starr. As with so many companies researched, it seems as though the company just evaporated. I remember several years ago in a magazine or glass journal I was reading, that the Peter, Peter shown here was patented, but never produced, while we had one sitting on our shelves even as I was reading the article.

Peter Peter Pumpkin Eater: Marked: "Vallona Star Design-Patent (c) 49 California"
$300.00 – $325.00
Squirrel on Stump: Marked: "Vallona-Starr 86 (c) 50 California"
Compare this jar with the Gilner one and they are basically the same except for lid.
$65.00 – $75.00

Man in the Moon: Marked: "Vallona Starr 302 (c) 51 California"
$260.00 – $290.00

WALT DISNEY

Walter Elias Disney was an American cartoonist and motion picture producer. Many popular cartoon characters and/or characters from movies Walt Disney produced have had cookie jars made in their likeness by pottery or ceramic companies. The most famous character who brought Walt Disney his fame was Mickey Mouse.

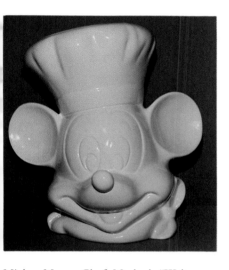

Mickey Mouse Chef: Marked: "Walt Disney Productions"
Believe this jar was sold through Disneyland.
$70.00 – $75.00

Mickey's Cookie Bus: Marked: "Walt Disney Productions Sears, Roebuck & Co. 1978"
$375.00 – $500.00
Pinocchio: Marked: "Walt Disney Productions"
$350.00 – $390.00

Alice in Wonderland: Marked: "Alice in Wonderland Walt Disney Productions"
$50.00 – $60.00
M.M. Head: (Leather Ears) Marked: "(c) Walt Disney Productions"
$375.00 – $410.00

WATT POTTERY

Globe Pottery, which began its business in 1905 in Crooksville, Ohio, was purchased by the Watt family and became Watt Pottery. In 1935, after making similar items such as stoneware crocks, with pot jars as their predecessor, the Watt Company began producing kitchen and ovenware. The kitchen and oven- ware was hand decorated from various patterns that had been designed. The company closed in 1965 after a fire destroyed the larger portion of the pottery and the owners chose not to rebuild. The remaining assets were sold.

Goodies: Marked: "Ovenware 72 USA"
$250.00 – $275.00
Apple: Marked: "Watt 503 USA Ovenware"
$330.00 – $360.00

Bleeding Heart: Marked: "Watt 76 USA Ovenware." I now believe this jar to be a bean pot instead of a cookie jar.
$100.00 – $110.00

WELLER POTTERY ———————————

Samuel Weller began making pottery in 1872 in Fultonham, Ohio. In 1882, he opened his first pottery which was in Zanesville, Ohio. His business was very prominent, although there were many other potteries in Zanesville. In 1890, Sam Weller built a three story plant and continued with his success. After his death in 1925, he was succeeded as president by his nephew, Harry Weller. Then came the depression years, creating less demand for pottery. Financial difficulties hit the pottery after World War II and the company leased some building space to Exxex Wire. In 1947, the Exxex Wire Company purchased the controlling stock and the Weller Pottery expired.

Pierre C.J.: Marked: "Weller Pottery since 1872"
$60.00 – $65.00

UNKNOWN AMERICAN MADE JARS ———————————

Gim-me Girl: Marked: "Helen's Gim-me #15 Helen Hetula"
$1,800.00 – $2,250.00

Tat-L-Tale: Marked: "Helen's Tat-L-Tale Original Helen Hetula"
This jar has the original label and it reads "I'm the original Tat-L-Tale Tilt My Head Up Side Down" This jar is very hard to find without finger broken off.
$1,600.00 – $1,800.00
Helen's Tat-L-Tale: Marked: "Helen's Tat-L-Tale Original Helen Hetula K 38"
This one has had the finger repaired. This jar comes in brown, and I have just a lid that has a flowered blouse.
$1,600.00 – $1,800.00

Wheel Barrow: Unmarked:
$45.00 – $55.00
Grandma: Unmarked:
$55.00 – $65.00

Snowman: Marked: "872" (This is a California Original)
$130.00 – $145.00
Monk with Key to Monastery: Unmarked:
I believe this jar to be made by same company who made the above grandma.
$65.00 – $75.00

Dog with Cookie: Unmarked:
$35.00 – $40.00
Private Property Dog House:
Unmarked:
$50.00 – $60.00

Topo Gigio (Mouse on the
Ed Sullivan Show) Marked:
"(c) Maria Perego
Distributed by Ross Products,
Inc. N.Y. 45-61"
$195.00 – $215.00
Toby Mug: Unmarked:
$55.00 – $65.00

Chef Head: Unmarked: Metlox
$150.00 – $175.00
Toby Mug: Unmarked:
$55.00 – $65.00

Two Story House:
Unmarked:
$30.00 – $35.00
Three Story House:
Unmarked:
$30.00 – $35.00

Smiling Elephant: Marked:
"(c) Bingo"
$45.00 – $50.00
Little Girl with Gingerbread
Man: Marked: "(c) Mopsy"
$50.00 – $60.00

Boy: Unmarked: (Very small jars)
$40.00 – $45.00
Girl: Unmarked:
$40.00 – $45.00

Train Engine:
Marked: "SC"
$90.00 – $100.00
Pinocchio and the
Whale: Unmarked:
$850.00 – $900.00

Astronaut Wizard:
Unmarked:
$125.00 – $150.00
Churn Boy: Unmarked:
$130.00 – $160.00

Shoe House: Unmarked:
$40.00 – $45.00
Gangster's Car:
Unmarked:
$55.00 – $65.00

Mammy–National Silver Company look-a-like: Unmarked:
$200.00 – $225.00
Chef–National Silver Company look-a-like: Unmarked:
$180.00 – $200.00

Bear with Cookie: Unmarked:
$35.00 – $38.00
Fish: Unmarked:
$35.00 – $40.00

Rabbi: Marked: "Designed in America by TSVI 384792"
$150.00 – $200.00
Rockingham Mammy: Unmarked:
$350.00 – $400.00

Dog: Unmarked:
$55.00 – $60.00
Coo Coo Clock: Unmarked:
$55.00 – $65.00

Sleepy Elephant: (Same mold
as California Orig. So?)
Unmarked:
$80.00 – $90.00
Rolling Pin: Unmarked:
$35.00 – $40.00

Dutch Lady: Unmarked:
$150.00 – $175.00
Dutch Man: Unmarked:
$150.00 – $175.00
Same Company made these jars as
made the following four jars.

Pilgrim or Quaker Lady:
Unmarked:
$150.00 – $175.00
Pilgrim or Quaker Man:
Unmarked:
$150.00 – $175.00

Pilgrim or Quaker Lady: Unmarked:
$150.00 – $175.00
Pilgrim or Quaker Man: Unmarked:
$150.00 – $175.00

Churn Boy: Unmarked:
$75.00 – $90.00
This churn boy different than
American Bisque or Regal.
Girl Scout Cookie Jar: Unmarked:
(Girl Scout Head and wording on jar)
$75.00 – $100.00

Clock: Unmarked:
$35.00 – $40.00
Clock: Unmarked:
$28.00 – $32.00

Dog Biscuit Jar: Unmarked,
except for "Lassie" written
on cookies.
$35.00 – $40.00
Farm Scene: Unmarked:
$70.00 – $95.00

Cottage with Lots & Lots of
Gold Trim: Unmarked:
$60.00 – $75.00
Cinderella: Unmarked:
I have always thought this jar
to be a Shawnee, if you check
out the colors and glaze. This
jar was also made with cold
paint, as was the Shawnee
pigs and Jack & Jill.
$190.00 – $215.00

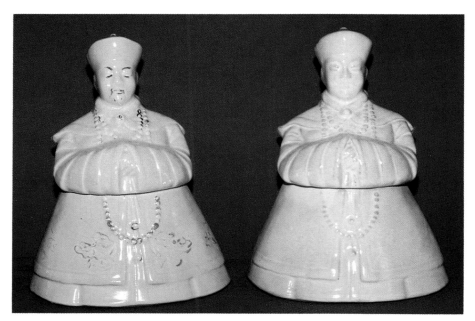

Oriental Man: Unmarked:
$65.00 – $75.00
Oriental Man: Unmarked:
$65.00 – $75.00

Clown with Drum: Unmarked:
$125.00 – $150.00
Poodle Head: Unmarked: Pfaltzgraf
Morton $32.00 – $38.00

Hippo: Marked: "California"
$150.00 – $175.00
Gingerbread Boy: Marked: "5541
USA"
$55.00 – $60.00

Springwater Cookie Company: Unmarked as far as maker of jar. $30.00 – $38.00
Luzianne Mammy: This is the original one! Marked: "U.S.A." $1,200.00 – $1,500.00
Paint has washed off. The jar approx. 12 inches tall.

Mammy: Unmarked by manufacturer, but marked by retail store which is "11 Jan 3 $1.19"
$150.00 – $175.00
Chef: Unmarked by manufacturer, but again $1.19
$150.00 – $175.00

New Orleans Mammy with Hominy Grits: Unmarked: $140.00 – $150.00
Aunt Jemima: (Plastic) Unmarked: (except for apron) $200.00 – $225.00

Young Black Man: (Who looks as if he's dressed up for a day at the Kentucky Derby) This jar is Majolica pottery. Marked: "4410" also "27." The picture here does not do the jar justice, although it has a damaged hat. If perfect–$2,200.00 – $2,500.00

Mammy: Unmarked by manufacturer, but has "$1.29 11 Jan 2" which was probably marked on it by retail store.
$125.00 – $130.00

Snowman: Marked: "(c) BC"
$35.00 – $40.00
Snowman: Unmarked:
$40.00 – $45.00

Square Jar with Handle: Unmarked:
$35.00 – $50.00
Man's Head: Unmarked: (Possibly Roseville Pottery)
$125.00 – $140.00

Unknown Jerome: Unmarked as far as jar manufacturer: $38.00 – $42.00
Twix: Unmarked as far as jar manufacturer: $38.00 – $42.00
These jars were used in stores to sell individual cookies to customers.

Haggard's Cookies: Plastic with tin lid & bottom. Marked: "Show Box St. Louis Missouri" $80.00 – $90.00
Dad's Oatmeal: Plastic with tin lid & bottom. Marked: "Weinman Bros Boxes Chco USA" $50.00 – $60.00
There are also two different sizes of Dad's glass jars. One is pictured in my first book and has wording on front of jar, but a smaller jar has the wording on the bottom.

Flower & Fruit Design: Unmarked: $15.00 – $18.00
Flower & Fruit Design: Unmarked: $15.00 – $18.00

Flower & Fruit Design: Unmarked:
$12.00 – $15.00
Daisy Design: Unmarked:
$12.00 – $15.00

Flower Design: Unmarked:
$10.00 – $12.00
Run, run, as fast as you can, you can't
catch me I'm the Gingerbread Man.
$18.00 – $20.00

Flower & Fruit Design: Unmarked:
$15.00 – $18.00
Hansel & Gretel: Unmarked:
$20.00 – $25.00

Dutch Children: Unmarked:
$20.00 – $25.00
Picket Fence with Lamb, Rabbit, Ducks &
Flowers: Unmarked:
$28.00 – $34.00
Both of these jars are quite small. The picture
is taken close so you can see detail.

Brown Crockery: Unmarked:
$45.00 – $50.00
Blue Crockery: Unmarked:
$45.00 – $50.00

Sailor: Made for Sears, Roebuck and
Company: Unmarked:
$90.00 – $100.00
Bean Pot Type: Marked but illegible:
This jar is stoneware and the turkey almost
looks like a rock.
$120.00 – $140.00

Farmer Slopping the Hog:
Unmarked:
$35.00 – $40.00
Frenchman: Unmarked:
$50.00 – $60.00

Four of the five different
Churn Boys in our collection:
The other one is shown in
the unknown American
Made section. The one on
the left is Japan, second
from left American Bisque
Company, third from left
Regal and the one on the
right is unknown also.

The three McCoy
Turkeys shown for
comparison.

BRAZIL

Rocking Horse with Bear:
Unmarked, but box reads
"(c) 1988 Action Industries,
Inc. Made in Brazil for
Action International Ltd."
$60.00 – $65.00
Santa Claus: Marked: "Made
in Brazil"
$70.00 – $75.00

Coo Coo Bird: Marked: "Hand Painted Made
in Brazil"
$25.00 – $30.00
Boy Duck: Marked: "Hand Painted Made in
Brazil"
$25.00 – $30.00

Elephant: Marked: "Hand Painted Made in
Brazil"
$25.00 – $30.00
Mamma Bear with Baby: Marked: "Weiss
Hand Painted Made in Brazil"
$38.00 – $42.00

China

Plastic Dog: Marked: "Fun Damental Too. LTD. Huntington Valley Pa. USA." The original barking cookie jar: "Patent Pending (c) 1990 Manufactured in China"
$35.00 – $40.00
Plastic Pig: Marked: "Fun Damental Too LTD. Huntington Valley Pa. USA." The original oinking cookie jar: "Patent Pending (c) 1990 Manufactured in China"
$35.00 – $40.00

CZECHOSLOVAKIA

Lavender with Roses: Marked: "2305 Made in Czechoslovakia"
$18.00 – $22.00
Black, Red & White Striped: Marked: "Erphila Art Pottery Czech Slovakia #52"
$25.00 – $30.00
Silhouette: Marked: "Erphila Art Pottery Czecho, Slovakia 2957 2"
$50.00 – $55.00

ENGLAND

House: Marked: "Prince Kensington Made in England Cottage Ware Reg. No. 845007"
$40.00 – $45.00
English Bull Dog: Marked: "Made in England V4488"
$80.00 – $90.00

Biscuit/Cracker with Ship: Marked: "Empire
Shelton Ivory England"
$25.00 – $30.00

GERMANY

Floral Biscuit/Cracker Jar: Marked:
"SMF Germany Wheelock Black Forest
Hand Painted Pottery"
$22.00 – $28.00

Monk: Marked: "K 29 Made
in W. Germany 1757"
Note! This jar looks smaller
than it really is because of the
life size pumpkin.
$350.00 – $375.00
Pumpkin W Gold Trim:
Marked: "Waechtersback W.
Germany"
$50.00 – $55.00

Pig: Marked: "Italy"
$25.00 – $30.00
Cow: Marked: "Italy"
$25.00 – $30.00

Humpty Dumpty: Marked: "Made in Italy"
$90.00 – $100.00
Cookie Jar with Cookies: Marked: "Made in Italy"
$12.00 – $15.00

Bengal Tiger: Marked: "Made in Italy" "14"
$65.00 – $75.00

Black Cat Head: Unmarked: $50.00 – $65.00

Mammy: Marked: "Made in Japan" $515.00 – $565.00
Chef: Marked: "Made in Japan" $425.00 – $475.00

Cookie Castle: Marked:
"(c) 1961 NAPCO
Bedford Ohio A5286M"
$50.00 – $60.00
Pig with Rooster: Marked:
"Napco Ware C7601"
$35.00 – $50.00

Jar with Tulips: Marked: "Made in Japan"
$22.00 – $28.00
Clyinder Jar with Windmill Scene–Wicker
Handle: Marked: "Made in Japan"
$18.00 – $22.00

Gingerbread
House: Unmarked:
$18.00 – $22.00
Shoe House: Unmarked:
$15.00 – $18.00

Green Gingerbread House
with Icing Trim: Unmarked:
$18.00 – $22.00
Brown Gingerbread House:
Marked only with sticker,
"Royal Sealy Japan"
$15.00 – $18.00

Cookie-Go-Round: Marked:
(Torn sticker, but part
reads)"___Roberts Company
San Francisco Made in
Japan"
$25.00 – $28.00
Carousel: Marked: "C-
3295" Also sticker that reads
"Napco Ceramics Japan"
$32.00 – $36.00

Squirrel with Acorn: Marked: "Japan"
$15.00 – $20.00
Mamma with Baby Rabbit: Marked with
sticker only: "Made in Japan"
$70.00 – $75.00
(This jar and the following four jars have
plastic eyes that look real)

Wilbur Cat: Marked: (Sticker Only) "Made in Japan"
$90.00 – $100.00
Emily Cat: Marked: (Sticker Only) "Made in Japan"
$90.00 – $100.00

Country Girl: Marked: (Sticker Only) "Made in Japan"
$70.00 – $75.00
Mamma Bear with Baby: Marked: (Sticker Only) "Made in Japan"
$80.00 – $90.00

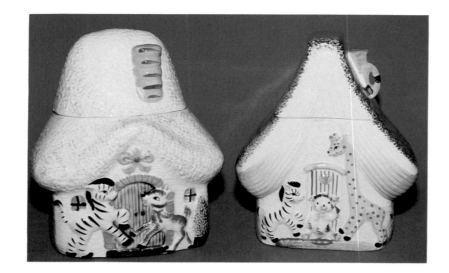

Zoo House: Marked: "G 9107"
$15.00 – $20.00
Zoo House: Marked: "B 315"
$15.00 – $20.00

Cinderella: Marked: "JC NAPCO 1957
K2292"
$210.00 – $260.00
Little Red Riding Hood: Marked: "JC
NAPCO 1957 K2292"
$210.00 – $260.00

Cherubs Around Apple Tree: Marked:
"Made in Japan"
$125.00 – $135.00
Dancing Under the Apple Tree: Marked:
"Made in Japan"
$60.00 – $75.00

Girl Panda: Marked: "Japan"
$12.00 – $15.00
Pirate: Unmarked:
$12.00 – $15.00

Santa's Toy Shop: Marked: "Japan"
$30.00 – $40.00
Igloo with Penguins: Marked: (Sticker
Only) "Enesco Imports Japan"
$45.00 – $50.00

Chorus Line Kittens: Unmarked:
$28.00 – $32.00
This Little Piggy Went to Market:
Unmarked:
$25.00 – $30.00

Scarecrow: Marked: "Japan"
$30.00 – $35.00
Clock: Marked: "(c) Enesco E-1034"
$30.00 – $35.00

Barn: Marked: (Sticker
Only) "Enesco Imports
Japan"
$20.00 – $25.00
Bakery with Sign: Marked:
"Enesco Imports Japan"
$12.00 – $15.00

Cookie Guard: Marked:
"(c) Enesco"
$20.00 – $25.00
Clown doing Backbend:
Marked: "Japan"
$45.00 – $50.00

Carousel: Marked: (Sticker Only) "Standard
Finest Specially Japan"
$20.00 – $25.00
Clown Head with Wicker Handle:
Unmarked:
$25.00 – $30.00

Churn Boy: Marked: "Made in Japan"
$60.00 – $70.00
Hen on Nest: Marked: "54/23"
$30.00 – $35.00

Pig with Scateboard: Marked: "Japan"
$15.00 – $18.00
Clown with Flower: Marked: "Japan"
$25.00 – $30.00

Tom & Jerry: Marked: "(c) Metro Goldwyn Mayer
Film Co."
$200.00 – $250.00
Tiger: Marked: "Made in Japan"
$20.00 – $25.00

Little Bo-Peep: Unmarked:
$200.00 – $250.00
Little Bo-Peep: Unmarked:
$200.00 – $250.00

Mother at Stove: Marked: "(c)
Sears, Roebuck and Co. 1978
Made in Japan"
$40.00 – $50.00
Cylinder with Windmill Scene:
Marked: "Japan"
$15.00 – $20.00

Hearts and Flowers: Marked:
"Tastesetter by Sigma Designed by
Nancie Goldstein"
$90.00 – $100.00
Lady Beauchamp: Marked:
"Lady Beauchamp from the Last
Elegant Bear Dennis Kyte for Sigma
the Tastesetter MCMLXV"
$60.00 – $65.00

Kilban Cats in Pants: Marked: "Sigma the
Tastesetter-designed by—" (Unreadable)
$75.00 – $85.00
Kabuki: Marked: "Kabuki (c) Sigma the Tastesetter"
$80.00 – $100.00

Vendor: Marked: (Label Only)
"Tastesetter by Sigma"
$100.00 – $125.00
Agatha: Marked: "Agatha Tastesetter
by Sigma Designed by David Straus"
$80.00 – $100.00

Beaver Fireman: Marked: "Cara Marks for Sigma the Tastesetter (R)"
$60.00 – $75.00
Kilban Cat with Guitar: Marked: "(c) Sigma The Tastesetter designed by B. Kilban"
$90.00 – $110.00

Victoria: Marked: "Victoria Tastesetter by Sigma"
$80.00 – $100.00
Senorita: Marked: "Siesta Tastesetter by Sigma Designed by David Straus"
$80.00 – $100.00

Famous Amos Cookies: Marked: "Sigma the Tastesetter"
$30.00 – $35.00
Kermit: Marked: "Sigma the Tastesetter (c) Henson Assoc."
$325.00 – $350.00

Santa on Motorcycle:
Marked: "F & F"
$375.00 – $400.00
Mrs. Santa: Marked: "F & F"
$115.00 – $150.00

Santa Claus: Marked: "(c) F.F.
1988"
$125.00 – $150.00
Witch: Marked: "Fitz & Floyd,
Inc. (c) MCMLXXX FF"
$275.00 – $300.00

Southwest Santa: Marked:
"(c) F. F. 1989"
$350.00 – $375.00
Cookie Bakery:
(Changeable Sign) Marked:
"(c) F.F."
$120.00 – $125.00

Pig: Marked: "(c) F F Fitz
and Floyd Inc. MCMLXXVI"
$55.00 – $65.00
Fat Cat: Marked: "Fat-Cat
Fitz and Floyd, Inc. (c)
MCMLXXVII F F"
$55.00 – $65.00

Rio Rita: Marked: "F F"
$140.00 – $165.00
Leap Frog: Marked: "Fitz &
Floyd, Inc. (c) MCMLXVII F F"
$55.00 – $65.00

Catarine the Great: Marked:
"Catarine the Great (c) F F
1990"
$160.00 – $170.00
Dinosaur: Marked: "(c) F F
1986"
$80.00 – $90.00

Racoon with Apple:
Marked: "FITZ &
FLOYD, INC (c)
MCMLXXIX FF"
$40.00 – $50.00
Lady Bear: Marked: "(c)
1991 F & F Taiwan"
$90.00 – $125.00

Scottish Miss: Marked: "1173" (Lefton China Jar)
$90.00 – $100.00
Winking Santa: Unmarked: (Lefton China)
$70.00 – $75.00

Chef Pig: Unmarked: (Lefton China)
$40.00 – $50.00
Snoopy: Marked: "Snoopy (c) 1958, 1966,
United Feature Syndicate, Inc."
$55.00 – $60.00

Lady Head: Marked: "geo z
Lefton 1957 040"
$40.00 – $45.00
Cat Head: Marked: "1502"
(Lefton China)
$40.00 – $45.00

Lady Head: Marked:
"geo z Lefton 1957"
$40.00 – $45.00
Yarn Pig: Unmarked:
$10.00 – $15.00

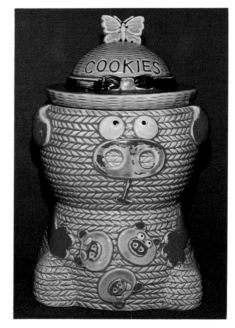

Blue Willow: Marked: (Sticker
Only) "Creative Imports, Inc.
Japan"
$45.00 – $50.00
Artist Painting a Nude:
Marked: "Made in Japan"
$125.00 – $150.00

Peasant People–Wicker Handle:
Unmarked:
$28.00 – $32.00
Windmill –Wicker Handle:
Unmarked:
$45.00 – $50.00

Dragon Jar with Gold Trim:
Wicker Handle: Marked:
"Made in Japan"
$35.00 – $40.00
Oriental Jar (with wrong lid):
Marked:
$15.00 – $18.00

Cookie Wagon: Unmarked:
$15.00 – $18.00
Circus Ring: Marked: "7636"
$15.00 – $18.00

Toaster: Marked: (Sticker Only) "Vandor (c) 1985 Made in Japan"
$90.00 – $100.00
Juke Box: Marked: (Sticker Only) "Vandor (c) 1985 Made in Japan"
$100.00 – $125.00

Howdy Doody in Bumper Car: Marked: "(c) 1988 Vandor"
$200.00 – $225.00

Betty Boop: Marked: "(c) 1985 King Features Syndicate, Inc."
$775.00 – $850.00
Howdy Doody: Unmarked:
$320.00 – $350.00

Chef Pig Head: Marked: PY (in a
circle)
$30.00 – $35.00
Musical Clown Head: Marked:
"Schmid Hand Painted (c) 1979"
$45.00 – $50.00
(Plays Candy Man)

Boy: Marked: "Grantcrest Hand
Painted Made in Japan"
$20.00 – $25.00
Granny: Marked: "Grantcrest
Hand Painted Made in Japan"
$20.00 – $25.00

Red Birds: Marked: (Sticker
Only) "Royal Sealy Japan"
$25.00 – $28.00
Mustache Cup with Barber
Shop Quartet: Marked:
(Sticker Only) "Enesco
Japan Imports" also stamped
"Enesco"
$45.00 – $50.00

Betsy Ross: Marked: "Japan"
$150.00 – $200.00
Kitchen Prayer: (Blue Dress)
Marked: "Japan"
$200.00 – $225.00

Pears and Grapes: Marked:
"53/865"
$12.00 – $15.00
Kitchen Prayer:
(Pink Dress) Unmarked: Note!
This jar has many accessories.
$200.00 – $225.00

Cards with Shoe
Finial: Unmarked:
$25.00 – $30.00
Boy with Helmet: Unmarked:
$20.00 – $25.00

Mouse on Clock: Unmarked:
$18.00 – $24.00
Monkey Getting into Cookies: Unmarked:
$25.00 – $30.00

Uncle Sam: Unmarked:
$50.00 – $75.00
Liberty Bell: Unmarked:
$25.00 – $35.00

Trudy Pig: Unmarked:
$60.00 – $65.00
Rudy (Rooty) Pig: Unmarked:
$60.00 – $65.00

Swan on Pond: Marked: "Japan"
$15.00 – $18.00
Sunflower: Unmarked:
$15.00 – $20.00

Bee on Bee Hive: Marked: (Sticker Only) "Josef
Originals"
$25.00 – $30.00
Cookie Panda: Unmarked:
$25.00 – $30.00

Green with Roses: Marked: "Japan"
$15.00 – $18.00
White with Roses: Marked: "Japan"
$25.00 – $28.00

Strawberries: Unmarked:
$25.00 – $30.00
Grapes: Unmarked:
$35.00 – $40.00

Mammy Stringholder: Marked: "Made in Japan"
$100.00 – $125.00
Mammy Cookie Jar: Marked: "Japan"
$900.00 – $1,000.00
Double Match Holder: Marked: "Made in Japan"
$200.00 – $225.00
Single Match Holder: Marked: "Made in Japan"
$175.00 – $200.00

Mamma Owl & Baby: Marked:
"Japan"
$35.00 – $40.00
Books: Marked: (Sticker Only)
"Enesco Imports Japan"
$20.00 – $25.00

Wild West with Horse Finial:
Unmarked:
$30.00 – $35.00
Clown: Unmarked:
$25.00 – $30.00

Clown Head: Marked: (Not very legible but
looks like. . .) "H3779"
$45.00 – $55.00
Clown Head: Marked: "60/153 Japan"
$38.00 – $42.00

Angel: Lid reverses: Angel side says: "Yes
Today you were an Angel" Unmarked:
$35.00 – $40.00
Love Birds: Marked: "Made in Japan"
$60.00 – $75.00

Devil: Lid reads "No! Today you
were a rascal" Same jar as
preceding angel.
$35.00 – $40.00
Dog in Basket: Marked: "Japan"
$25.00 – $30.00

Wise Owl: Marked: "Japan"
$30.00 – $35.00
Elephant: Marked: "Japan"
$30.00 – $35.00

Puppy: Marked: "Japan"
$30.00 – $35.00
Monk: Marked: "Japan"
$30.00 – $35.00

Rabbit: Marked: "Japan"
$30.00 – $35.00
Cat with Cookie: Marked: "Japan"
$30.00 – $35.00

Rabbit: Marked: "Japan"
$30.00 – $35.00
Lamb: Marked: "Japan"
$35.00 – $40.00

Owl Learning his ABC's: Marked: " Japan"
$30.00 – $35.00
Humpty Dumpty: Marked: "Japan"
$45.00 – $50.00

Peter Peter, Pumpkin Eater:
Marked: "Japan"
$70.00 – $80.00
Alice in Wonderland: Marked:
"Japan"
$70.00 – $80.00

Bamboo Look:
Unmarked:
$10.00 – $15.00
Rooster: Unmarked:
$12.00 – $18.00

Red & Blue Floral:
Marked: "Hand Painted
Made in Japan Patent
Applied For"
$25.00 – $30.00
Round Ball Shape with
Blue Birds: Marked:
"Japan"
$20.00 – $25.00

Cookie Talk: Marked: "Japan"
$18.00 – $22.00
Tea Kettle with Clock: Marked: "Japan"
$15.00 – $20.00

Santa with Candy Cane: Marked:
"Japan"
$35.00 – $40.00
Holiday Cookie Box: Marked: "Japan"
$30.00 – $35.00

Mr. Cool Penguin: Marked: "Japan"
$30.00 – $35.00
Turtle with Derby: Unmarked:
$30.00 – $35.00

Fruit Slices: Unmarked, but this jar National Silver Company of NAGOYA Japan"
$10.00 – $15.00
Lost Love: Marked: "KME 251"
$45.00 – $50.00

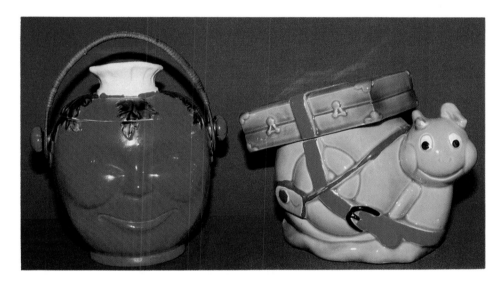

Tomato: Marked: "Hand Painted"
$20.00 – $25.00
Traveling Snail: Marked: "Japan"
$20.00 – $25.00

Parrot on Bananas: Marked: "E 0069"
$30.00 – $35.00
Studious Turtle: Marked: "Japan"
$20.00 – $25.00

Butler: Marked: "Japan"
$1,500.00 – $1,800.00
Mammy: Unmarked:
$725.00 – $775.00

Butler: (Note smaller size than
above jar) Marked: "Japan"
$1,000.00 – $1,200.00
Mammy: (Have seen this jar
marked with number) Unmarked:
$725.00 – $775.00

Southern Gentleman:
Unmarked:
$40.00 – $50.00
Vending Cart: Marked
but illegible:
$35.00 – $40.00

Lion with Racket: Marked: "Japan"
$20.00 – $25.00
Lion: Marked: "Japan"
$15.00 – $18.00

Bambi Look-a-Like, Racoon on Lid:
Unmarked:
$25.00 – $30.00
Puppy in Flower Bed: Unmarked:
$20.00 – $25.00

Betsy Baker: (Emblem for Roselyn Bakeries of
Indianapolis Indiana) Unmarked:
$60.00 – $75.00
Scottish Boy with Umbrella: Marked: "Made
in Japan Genuine Trudeau Product Montreal
Toronto Japan Gtc Japan"
$35.00 – $45.00

Alpine Girl: Marked: "Japan"
$30.00 – $35.00
Alpine Boy: Marked: "Japan"
$30.00 – $35.00

Campbell Kid: Nodder Jar:
Marked: "DAVAR"
$125.00 – $150.00
Chef Pig: Unmarked:
$35.00 – $40.00

Clown Bust: Marked: "PY
(within a circle) Japan"
$35.00 – $40.00
Clarabell (?) Clown: Marked:
"Design (c) Gibson Greeting
Cards, Inc" (Sticker "O M
Japan")
$100.00 – $125.00

Castle: Marked: (Sticker Only)
"Made in Japan"
$20.00 – $25.00
Cookie Car: Marked: "Japan"
$20.00 – $25.00

Engineer: Unmarked:
$20.00 – $25.00
Train Engine: Unmarked:
$20.00 – $25.00

Miss Cutie Pie: Marked: "NAPCO
Ceramics Japan" (sticker)– Miss
Cutie Pie" "A 35005/AL"
$65.00 – $75.00
Musical Boy-Chef Head: Marked:
"Japan"
$80.00 – $100.00

Japan

Girl with Grapes—Bluebirds
Finial: Marked: "Arcadia
#C6672"
$25.00 – $28.00
Cat with Mouse: Unmarked:
$25.00 – $30.00

Scarecrow: Unmarked:
$30.00 – $35.00
Cow: Marked: "Japan"
$38.00 – $42.00

Fire Plug: Marked: (Sticker
Only) "Fred Roberts
Company Made in Japan"
$30.00 – $35.00
Alpo Dog: OOPS—Goofed:
Should be with USA jars, but
since I missed the right
category, hope I'll be
forgiven if I put him with a
fire plug.
$65.00 – $70.00

Owl in Hollow Tree:
Marked: "Japan"
$15.00 – $20.00
Wildlife: Unmarked:
$15.00 – $20.00

Wildlife #2: Unmarked:
Note! Although one can't tell much by looking at this picture, the two outer deer legs are not molded up against the jar, but stand out separately and could be broken very easily.
$40.00 – $50.00
Cookie Carousel: Unmarked:
$22.00 – $28.00

Cowboy: Note the name Tom & Jerry on the lid:
Marked: "Japan"
$60.00 – $65.00
Slot Machine: Marked: "1979 Cara Creations Corp. Made in Japan"
$30.00 – $35.00

Merry-Go-Round:
Unmarked:
$30.00 – $35.00
Basketweave with
Cookies: Unmarked:
$12.00 – $15.00

Bear: (Charcoal color)
Marked: (Sticker Only)
"Enesco Imports Japan"
$20.00 – $25.00
Bear Stealing Cookie:
Marked: (Sticker Only)
"Enesco Imports Japan"
$18.00 – $22.00

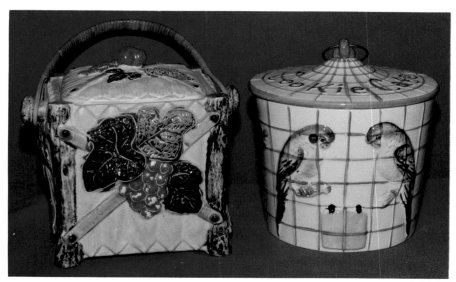

Grapes on Trellis: Marked:
"Made in Japan"
$25.00 – $30.00
A previous owner of this jar had
written July 31, 1937, on this
jar.
Parrots or Parakeets in Cage:
Unmarked:
$40.00 – $50.00

Merry-Go-Round: Unmarked:
$30.00 – $35.00
Dutch Kids on Windmill:
Marked: "Tulip Tyme 8926Y"
$65.00 – $70.00

Fireman Elephant: Marked: "Japan"
$35.00 – $40.00
Mary and her Little Lamb: Marked: "Vicki
Japan"
$45.00 – $50.00

Clown with Cookie Basket:
Marked: "Japan"
$25.00 – $35.00
Clown: Unmarked:
$25.00 – $30.00

Japan

Duck with Bonnet: Marked: "Japan"
$25.00 – $30.00
Penguin: Unmarked:
$25.00 – $30.00

Dutch Girl: Marked: "2366"
$60.00 – $65.00
(Probably Lefton China Mark)
Here Comes Trouble: Marked: "Enesco
Imports Japan" The jar has a girl mate.
$80.00 – $90.00

Raggedy Ann: Marked: "C8824"
$45.00 – $50.00
Raggedy Andy: Marked: "C8824"
$45.00 – $50.00

Pink Pig: Marked: "Gifts Around the World Made in Japan"
$15.00 – $20.00
Cat on Cookie Box: Marked: "Vicki Japan"
$25.00 – $30.00

Treasure Chest: Unmarked:
$25.00 – $30.00
Granny: Unmarked:
$20.00 – $25.00

Square Dance Scene: Marked: "C1978-Enesco E 1037"
$30.00 – $35.00
A Gathering of Men: Marked: "Made in Japan"
$32.00 – $38.00

Miss Lemon: Marked: "MIYAO"
$20.00 – $25.00
Mr. Red Pepper: Marked: "Made in Japan"
$20.00 – $25.00

Fireplug Police: Unmarked:
$20.00 – $25.00
Clown Selling Cookies: Marked: "Japan"
$35.00 – $40.00

House with Thatched Roof: Marked:
"53/909"
$20.00 – $25.00
Round House with Thatched Roof: Marked:
"Made in SS Japan"
$25.00 – $28.00

Chinese Lady: Marked: "Made in Japan"
$80.00 – $90.00
Lily (or Flag): Marked: "Made in Japan"
$15.00 – $18.00

Santa in Snowball: Unmarked: This could
possibly be homemade ceramic piece.
$20.00 – $25.00
Lion: Marked: "C2477"
$15.00 – $18.00

Musical Teddy Bear: Plays Teddy Bears Picnic:
Marked: (Sticker Only) "Made in Japan"
$35.00 – $40.00
Cooky Can: Marked: (Sticker Only) "Enesco
Imports Japan"
$12.00 – $15.00

White Daisies: Unmarked:
$10.00 – $12.00
Crowing Rooster: Unmarked:
$15.00 – $18.00

Little Black Girl: Marked: "(c)
Sears, Roebuck and Co. 1978
Japan"
$700.00 – $800.00
Begging Dog: Unmarked:
$26.00 – $36.00

Clown Riding Elephant: Marked:
"C1957 Yona Original"
$100.00 – $125.00
Clowns with Drum: Marked:
"Japan"
$35.00 – $40.00

Dog with Cake: Marked: "Japan"
$18.00 – $22.00
Dog with Bow: Marked: "Japan"
$18.00 – $22.00

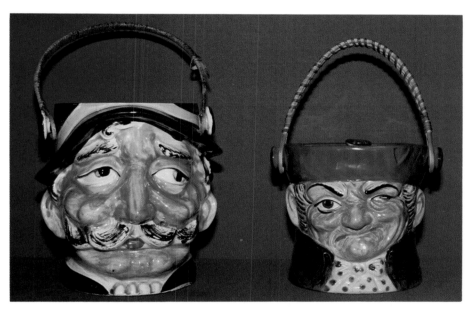

Englishman: (This one minus hat) Marked: "Hand Painted Japan"
$40.00 – $48.00
Toby Head: Marked: "MK"
$38.00 – $44.00

Fox Hunt Scene: Unmarked:
$12.00 – $15.00
Wells Fargo Co.: Unmarked:
$12.00 – $15.00

George Washington: Marked:
"Made in Japan"
$30.00 – $40.00
Cottage: Marked: "Occupied
Japan"
$60.00 – $70.00

KOREA

Michaelangelo Ninja Turtle: Marked:
"International Silver Co. Made in Korea
1990 Merage Studios. Exclusively
Licensed by Surge Licensing Co." Do
Not Wash in Dishwasher:
$45.00 – $50.00
Donatello: Marked: Same as Michaelangelo:
$45.00 – $50.00

Funshine Bear: Marked: "Funshine Bear
TM One of the Care Bears MCMLXXXV
American Greeting Corp: Cleveland Ohio
44144 Made in Korea 53044"
$70.00 – $80.00
Tenderheart Bear: Marked the same as
Funshine except for the name "Funshine"
$70.00 – $80.00

Bird House: Marked:
"Hearth and Home
Designs (c) H & HD"
$35.00 – $40.00
Mother Cat with Kittens:
Marked: Same as Bird House:
$28.00 – $36.00

Winking Clown: Marked:
(Sticker Only) "Made in
Mexico"
$25.00 – $30.00
Leopard: Marked: (Sticker
Only) "Hand Painted" &
"Made in Mexico"
$30.00 – $36.00

Snowman: Marked: (Sticker Only)
"Made in Mexico"
$50.00 – $55.00
Snowlady: Marked: (Sticker Only)
"Made in Mexico"
$50.00 – $55.00

Mexico

Bridesmaid:
Marked: "Hearth & Home Designs (c) H & HD Made in Mexico"
$35.00 – $40.00
Carousel Horse:
Marked: "Hearth & Home Designs (c) H & HD"
$40.00 – $50.00

PORTUGAL

Dog with Cookie: Marked with sticker only: "Made in Portugal Over and Back, Inc. Surveyors to the World"
$30.00 – $40.00
Sailboat: Marked with sticker only: "M. Kamentstein, Inc. (c) MCMLXXXIV Made in Portugal"
$45.00 – $60.00

TAIWAN

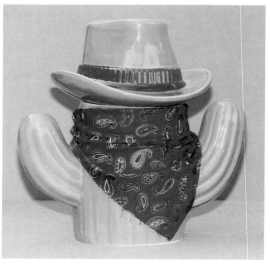

Cactus Bandit: Marked with sticker only: "Made in Taiwan Clay Art San Francisco '89"
$28.00 – $32.00

Michelangelo: Marked: "Taiwan"
(Incised) also label "Teenage Mutant
Ninja Turtles (c) 1990 Merage Studios
USA Exclusively Licensed by Surge
Licensing, Inc. International Silver
Company Made in Taiwan"
$45.00 – $50.00
Donatello: Marked the same as
Michelangelo:
$45.00 – $50.00

Cool Cookie: Marked: "Made in Taiwan" (c) 1981
Hallmark Cards, Inc. $1,600.00 – $1,800.00
Cookie Bandit: Marked: "Made in Taiwan" (c)
1981 Hallmark Cards, Inc.
$700.00 – 1,000.00
Cookie jars of Hallmark's famous Shirt Tales
characters, the Penguin (Cool Cookie) and the
Raccoon (Cookie Bandit), were made in test runs
of 200 each. The Raccoon was reordered in the
amount of 3500, making a total of 3700 before
transportation. The Penguin, which was not a good
seller, was not reordered, which accounts for the
rarity of this jar.

Pound Puppy: Marked: "Pound Puppies
Exclusively Distributed By United Silver
& Cutlery Co. (c)1987 Tonka Corp Made
in Taiwan"
$60.00 – $70.00
Kitchen Witch: Unmarked:
$20.00 – $28.00

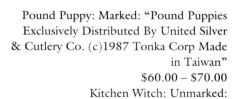

Pound Puppy:
Marked same as puppy on page 241:
$60.00 – $70.00
Ernie the Keebler Elf: Marked: "(c) 1989 Keebler Company" Also sticker "Made in Taiwan"
$50.00 – $55.00

Human Bean: Marked: "Human Beans (c) 1981 Morgan, Inc. Lic. Enesco Imports"
$40.00 – $50.00
Praying Girl: Marked: "Dear God Kids (c) 1982 Intercontinental Licensee Enesco" Also sticker "Enesco Designed Giftware Taiwan"
$75.00 – $85.00

Cat with Flower Basket: Marked: (Sticker Only) "Made in Taiwan"
$38.00 – $42.00
Florist Shop: Marked: (Sticker Only) "Made in Taiwan"
$32.00 – $36.00

Mrs. Fields Cookies: Marked: (Sticker Only) "Made in Taiwan"
$35.00 – $40.00
Nite-Time Bear: Marked: (Sticker Only) "Made in Taiwan"
$30.00 – $35.00

City Rat: Marked: (Sticker Only) "Made in Taiwan"
$20.00 – $25.00
Blue Bonnet Sue: Marked: "(c) 1989 Nabisco" (Also Sticker) "Made in Taiwan"
$40.00 – $45.00

Nerd with Ball Cap: Marked: "Nerds (c) 1984 Willy Wonka Brands exclusively distributed by United Silver & Cutlery Co. Made in Taiwan"
$40.00 – $45.00
Nerd on Skateboard: Marked: Same as Nerd with Ball Cap:
$40.00 – $45.00

Santa Nerd: Marked: Same as nerds on page 243.
$40.00 – $45.00
Snoopy: Marked: "Snoopy (c) 1958, 1966 United Feature Syndicate, Inc. Willets Designs: Made in Taiwan"
$115.00 – $130.00

Bears Decorating Christmas Tree: Marked: (Sticker Only) The Cooks Bazaar Made in Taiwan"
$50.00 – $60.00
Tricycle R. V.: Marked: "The Cooks Bazaar Made in Taiwan"
$20.00 – $25.00

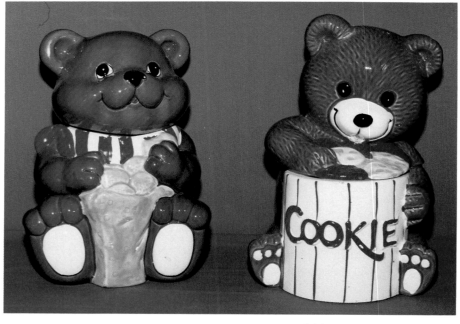

Bear with Sack of Cookies: Unmarked:
$15.00 – $18.00
Bear with Cookie Jar: Marked: "Welcome Taiwan"
$15.00 – $18.00

Boy with Cookie Jar:
Unmarked:
$18.00 – $22.00
Santa with Bear: Marked:
"Welcome Taiwan"
$30.00 – $35.00

Bartender Alligator: Marked:
(Sticker Only) "Made in Taiwan"
$30.00 – $35.00
Milk Bone Jar for Dog Treats:
Marked: "N2922 (Sticker) R.R.
Roman Made in Taiwan"
$55.00 – $65.00

Gone with the Wind Mammy:
Marked with sticker only: "Gone
with the Wind H4115 Distributed
by the Heirloom Tradition A
Division of Hamilton Gifts (c)
1939 Seiznick Ren 1967 MGM
1990 Turner Entertainment Co.
All Rights Reserved Made in
Taiwan"
Note! This jar was originally done
with some cold paint.
$115.00 – $125.00
Emmit Kelly Jr.: Marked: "The
Emmet Kelly Jr. (R) Collection
Exclusively from Flambro"
$500.00 – $550.00

Mother & Baby Bear: Unmarked:
$15.00 – $18.00
Spuds Look-A-Like: Unmarked: **Note!**
Wrong eye is black.
$65.00 – $75.00

Nutcracker
Nutcracker: Marked: (Sticker Only)
"Made in Taiwan"
$35.00 – $40.00
Nutcracker
Nutcracker: Marked: (Sticker Only)
"Made in Taiwan"
$35.00 – $40.00

Santa with Spiral Cap: Unmarked:
(There is a Mrs. to match)
$30.00 – $35.00
Alligator with Cookie: Unmarked: This jar
has a wooden dial at the back of his
mouth where the lid will open slightly or
lift off.
$60.00 – $65.00

Sprout marked: "The Pillsbury
Company Made in Taiwan"
$40.00 – $45.00
Clown marked (sticker only):
"made in Thailand"
$40.00 – $45.00

UNKNOWN FOREIGN JARS

Santa with Candy Cane:
Unmarked:
$25.00 – $30.00
Bear in Car: Unmarked:
$50.00 – $60.00

Crocodile: Unmarked: $25.00 – $35.00
Crocodile Mailman: Unmarked: $30.00 – $35.00

Trapper Bear: Unmarked: $40.00 – $50.00
Flop Eared Bear: Unmarked: $22.00 – $25.00 possibly American made

PLASTIC JARS

Santa Head: Marked: "(c) Carolina
Enterprises 1973 Tarboro N. Enterprises
Made in USA 024288"
$20.00 – $30.00
Santa Head: Unmarked:
$45.00 – $50.00

Cookie Hour: Unmarked:
$20.00 – $25.00
Ball Shape: Marked: "The Burrought
Co. LA USA No. 125 Burrite"
$15.00 – $18.00

Michelangelo: "R & (c) Mirage Studios
Teenage Mutant Ninja Turtles All Rights
Reserved Exclusively Licensed by Surge
Licensing"
$10.00 – $15.00
Donatello: Marked, same as Michelangelo:
Note! These turtles were sold at K-Mart
Stores in 1991 filled with Chocolate Chip
Cookies and sold for $3.98 plus tax. They are
meant for a bank as they have a place for a slot
to be cut in the back, however, many are
collecting these for cookie jars too.
$10.00 – $15.00

Mickey's 50th Anniversary: "(c) Walt Disney Productions" Tin made by "Cheinco Housewares J Chein & Co. Burlington N. J. 08076"
$50.00 – $60.00
Mickey and his Friends: Marked same as 50th Anniversary.
$35.00 – $40.00

Mickey Mouse Club: Marked same as above two tins.
$60.00 – $80.00
Clowns with Balloons: Marked: "Ballon of Cleveland Ohio 44118 Made in USA"
$10.00 – $15.00

Cookies and Milk and Lots of Sunshine: Marked: "Ransburg Indianapolis Made in USA Trademark"
$10.00 – $12.00
Gold Medal Cookies: Marked: Same as Cookies & Milk Tin.
$20.00 – $25.00

Grandma's Cookies: Unmarked except what
is on front of can: $10.00 – $12.00
Man with Scythe Cutting Wheat: Marked:
(Sticker Only) "Made in USA by Kromex"
$8.00 – $10.00

Two Chefs with BIG Cookie: Marked:
"Weibro Chicago USA"
$35.00 – $42.00
Blue Willow: Marked: "Krispy Kan The
Luce Corp. South Norwalk, Conn US
Pat. No. 2548168"
$35.00 – $42.00

Raggedy Ann and Andy Tin: Marked:
"Randsburg Indianapolis Made in
USA"
$10.00 – $12.00
Kids Hanging Cookie Sign: Marked:
"Webro Chicago USA"
$15.00 – $20.00

Cookie Tins

Newspaper Print: Marked: "Blue Magic Krispy Kan The Luce Corp. Conn. US Pat No. 2548618" $22.00 – $26.00
Home Style Cookies: Marked: "Balloon of Cleveland Ohio 44118 Made in USA" $8.00 – $10.00

Clown Face: Marked, but illegible: $10.00 – $12.00
Cookies & Milk: Marked, but illegible: $8.00 – $10.00

Barnums Animals: (Small tin) Marked: "Replica 1914 Designs" $12.00 – $16.00
Nestles Toll House: (Small tin) Unmarked: $15.00 – $18.00
Nestles 50th Anniversary: Unmarked: $15.00 – $18.00

Old MacDonald's Farm Musical Tin: Marked with Sticker: "Musical Tin Plays Old MacDonald Had A Farm 10,000 Times Danish Butter Cookies. Dist. by Festival Foods Corp." $25.00 – $35.00

Circus Tent: Marked: "Balloon of Cleveland Ohio 44118 Made in USA" $8.00 – $10.00

CERAMIC CLASS JARS

I personally do not care for cookie jars made in ceramic classes, however I do have three or four in my collection. I bought the Santa going over his list, sight unseen, from a dealer from another state thinking it was a company made jar. My husband and I have four grandchildren, so I do display the two Santas below at Christmas time.

Santa, going over his list: Mark: "Alberta Mold Co." on bottom of jar.
$65.00 – $75.00
Santa, reading note from child: Marked: D & B Originals
$80.00 – $100.00

Kangaroo: Mark: "Arnells Mold Co."
$50.00 – $55.00
Devil on Money Sack: Although the picture is too dark to read the writing on jar, it reads "Money Root of All Evil"
$60.00 – $65.00

BIBLIOGRAPHY

Coats, Pamela. *The Real McCoy*. Des Moines, IA: Wallace-Homestead, 1971.

Coats, Pamela. *The Real McCoy Volume II*. Indianapolis, IN: 1974.

Coats, Pamela. *The Real McCoy Bi-Centennial Price Guide Volume II½*. Indianapolis, IN: 1976.

Derwich, Jenny B. and Dr. Mary Latos, *Dictionary Guide to United States Pottery & Porcelain (19th and 20th Century)*. Jenstan of Franklin, MI: 1984.

Felker, Sharon L. *Lovely Hull Pottery*. Des Moines, IA: Wallace-Homestead, 1974.

Nichols, Harold. *McCoy Cookie Jars from the First to the Latest*. Lake Mills, IA: Nichols Publishing. Printed by Graphic Publishing Company, 1987.

Paul, E. and A. Petersen. *Collector's Handbook to Marks On Porcelain And Pottery*. Green Farms, CT: Modern Books and Crafts, Inc., 1974.

Rehl, Norma and Connie DeAngelo. *Abingdon Pottery*. Milford, NJ: 1981.

Schneider, Mike. *The Complete Cookie Jar Book*. West Chester, PA: Schiffer Publishing Ltd., 1991.

Chipman, Jack. *Collector's Encyclopedia of California Pottery*. Paducah, KY: Collector Books, 1992.

Cunningham, Jo. *The Collector's Encyclopedia of American Dinnerware*. Paducah, KY: Collector Books, 1982.

DePasquale, Dan & Gail and Larry Peterson. *Red Wing Collectibles*. Paducah, KY: Collector Books, 1985.

DePasquale, Dan & Gail and Larry Peterson. *Red Wing Stoneware*. Paducah, KY: Collector Books, 1983.

Huxford, Sharon & Bob. *The Collector's Encyclopedia of Brush McCoy Pottery*. Paducah, KY: Collector Books, 1978.

Huxford, Sharon & Bob. *The Collector's Encyclopedia of McCoy Pottery*. Paducah, KY: Collector Books, 1978.

Huxford, Sharon & Bob. *The Collector's Encyclopedia of Roseville Pottery*. Paducah, KY: Collector Books, 1976.

Huxford, Sharon & Bob. *The Collector's Encyclopedia of Weller Pottery*. Paducah, KY: Collector Books, 1979.

Lehner, Lois. *Lehner's Encyclopedia of U.S. Marks on Pottery, Porcelain & Clay*. Paducah, KY: Collector Books, 1988.

Roberts, Brenda. *The Collector's Encyclopedia of Hull Pottery*. Paducah, KY: Collector Books, 1980.

Roerig, Fred and Joyce Herndon. *The Collector's Encyclopedia of Cookie Jars*. Paducah, KY: Collector Books, 1991.

Simon, Delores. *Red Wing Pottery with Rumrill*. Paducah, KY: Collector Books, 1980.

Simon, Delores. *Shawnee Pottery*. Paducah, KY: Collector Books, 1977.

Whitmyer, Margaret & Kenn. *The Collector's Encyclopedia of Hall China*. Paducah, KY: Collector Books, 1989.

INDEX BY SHAPE